Grammar
Mate 1

저자 약력

이강희   (전) 한국 외국어대학교 외국어연수 평가원 영어 전임 강사
하와이 주립대 Second Language Studies 석사
한국 외국어대학교 영어과 학사
〈Grammar's Cool〉 (YBM), 〈빠르게 잡는 유형독해 Level 2〉 (천재교육)
〈New TOEIC 콩나물 Basic Listening〉 (두산동아), 〈TOEIC CLINIC Beginner〉 (위트앤위즈덤) 등 다수의 교재 공저

전지원   미국 오리건 주립대 Linguistics 석사
(현) 한국 외국어대학교 외국어연수 평가원 영어 전임 강사
〈내공 중학 영작문〉 (다락원), 〈Grammar plus Writing〉 (다락원), 〈Grammar plus Writing Start〉 (다락원),
〈Grammar's Cool〉 (YBM), 〈빠르게 잡는 영문법〉 (천재교육) 등 다수의 교재 공저

박혜영   미국 하와이 주립대 Second Language Studies 석사
(현) 한국 외국어대학교 외국어연수 평가원 영어 전임 강사
〈내공 중학 영작문〉 (다락원), 〈Grammar plus Writing〉 (다락원), 〈Grammar plus Writing Start〉 (다락원),
〈Grammar's Cool〉 (YBM), 〈빠르게 잡는 영문법〉 (천재교육) 등 다수의 교재 공저

Grammar Mate ❶

지은이   이강희, 전지원, 박혜영

펴낸이   정규도
펴낸곳   (주)다락원

초판 1쇄 발행   2020년 2월 10일
초판 4쇄 발행   2023년 5월 8일

편집   서정아, 서민정, 김민아
디자인   구수정
삽화   오영남
영문 감수   Michael A. Putlack

다락원 경기도 파주시 문발로 211
내용문의 (02)736-2031 내선 503
구입문의 (02)736-2031 내선 250~252

Fax (02)732-2037
출판등록 1977년 9월 16일 제 406-2008-000007호

ISBN   978-89-277-0872-8 64740
            978-89-277-0871-1 64740(set)

http://www.darakwon.co.kr
다락원 홈페이지를 방문하시면 상세한 출판정보와 함께
동영상강좌, MP3 자료 등 다양한 어학 정보를 얻으실 수 있습니다.

Grammar
Mate 1

DARAKWON

Introduction

Grammar Mate 시리즈는

Core basic English grammar

초급 학습자들에게 꼭 필요한 핵심 문법 사항을 수록하여 영문법의 기초를
탄탄히 다질 수 있도록 하였습니다.

Easy, clear explanations of grammar rules and concepts

문법 개념과 용어를 쉽고 명료하게 설명하였습니다. 포괄적인 문법 설명을 지양하고
세분화된 단원 구성과 포인트 별 핵심 설명으로 확실한 이해를 도울 수 있도록 하였습니다.

Plenty of various step–by-step exercises

다양하고 풍부한 연습 문제를 제공합니다. 지나친 drill이나 서술형 등 한쪽으로
치우친 유형이 아닌, 개념 이해부터 적용까지 체계적이고 다양한 문제 풀이를 통해
자연스럽게 문법 개념을 익힐 수 있습니다.

Writing exercises to develop writing skills and grammar accuracy

문법 학습 후 문장 쓰기 연습을 통해 내신 서술형에 대비할 수 있습니다.
또한 영어 문장을 써봄으로써 답을 맞추기 위한 문법이 아니라 영어라는 큰 틀 안에서
문법을 정확히 활용할 수 있도록 하였습니다.

Comprehensive tests to prepare for actual school tests

각 CHAPTER가 끝날 때마다 실제 학교 내신 시험에서 출제되는 문제 유형들로 구성된
테스트를 제공하여 학교 내신 시험에 익숙해질 수 있도록 하였습니다.

Workbook for further practice

워크북을 통한 추가 문제를 제공함으로써 문법 개념을 숙지할 때까지
충분한 문제와 복습 컨텐츠를 제공합니다.

How to Use This Book

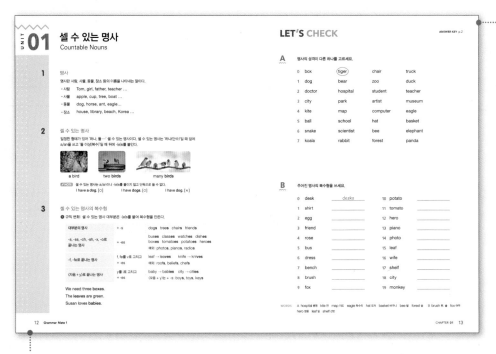

LET'S CHECK

왼쪽 페이지에서 학습한 내용을 개념 확인 문제를 통해 바로 연습해볼 수 있습니다.

GRAMMAR POINT

초급자가 알아야 할 문법 사항을 도표, 사진, 실용적인 예문을 통해 이해하기 쉽게 설명하였습니다.
주의해야 할 사항은 **NOTE** 로, 더 알아야 할 사항은 **+PLUS** 로 제시하였습니다.

LET'S PRACTICE

보다 풍부한 연습 문제를 통해 문법 실력을 다질 수 있습니다.

LET'S WRITE

문법 사항을 문장 쓰기에
적용해봄으로써 학습 효과를
증대시키고 내신 서술형에
대비할 수 있습니다.
빈칸 완성, 어구 배열, 영작하기
문제로 구성되어 있습니다.

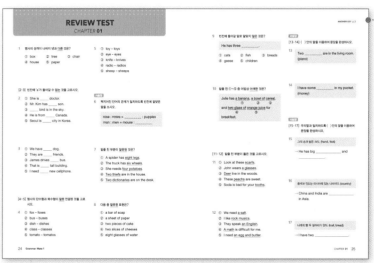

REVIEW TEST

각 CHAPTER가 끝날 때마다
학습한 문법 사항을 총 정리할
수 있고, 나아가 실제 내신 문제
유형에 익숙해질 수 있습니다.

WORKBOOK

워크북을 통해 학습한 해당
UNIT의 문법사항을 다시 한번
복습하며 실력을 점검해볼 수
있습니다.

Contents

CHAPTER
01

Nouns
명사

LET'S LOOK

a banana

apples

milk

명사란 사람, 사물, 동물, 장소 등의 이름을 나타내는 말이다.
영어에서 명사는 크게 **셀 수 있는 명사**와 **셀 수 없는 명사**로 나눌 수 있다.

01 셀 수 있는 명사
Countable Nouns

1 명사

명사란 사람, 사물, 동물, 장소 등의 이름을 나타내는 말이다.

- 사람　　Tom, girl, father, teacher …
- 사물　　apple, cup, tree, boat …
- 동물　　dog, horse, ant, eagle…
- 장소　　house, library, beach, Korea …

2 셀 수 있는 명사

일정한 형태가 있어 '하나, 둘 …' 셀 수 있는 명사이다. 셀 수 있는 명사는 '하나(단수)'일 때 앞에
a/an을 쓰고 '둘 이상(복수)'일 때 뒤에 -(e)s를 붙인다.

a bird　　　　　　**two birds**　　　　　　　**many birds**

> **✎ NOTE**　셀 수 있는 명사는 a/an이나 -(e)s를 붙이지 않고 단독으로 쓸 수 없다.
> I have **a dog**. [○]　　　　I have **dogs**. [○]　　　　I have **dog**. [×]

3 셀 수 있는 명사의 복수형

❶ 규칙 변화: 셀 수 있는 명사 대부분은 -(e)s를 붙여 복수형을 만든다.

대부분의 명사	+ -s	dog**s** tree**s** chair**s** friend**s**
-s, -ss, -ch, -sh, -x, -o로 끝나는 명사	+ -es	bus**es** class**es** watch**es** dish**es** box**es** tomato**es** potato**es** hero**es** 예외: photo**s**, piano**s**, radio**s**
-f, -fe로 끝나는 명사	f, fe를 v로 고치고 + -es	leaf → lea**ves**　　knife → kni**ves** 예외: roof**s**, belief**s**, chef**s**
〈자음 + y〉로 끝나는 명사	y를 i로 고치고 + -es	baby → bab**ies**　city → cit**ies** 〈모음 + y〉는 + -s: boy**s**, toy**s**, key**s**

We need three **boxes**.

The **leaves** are green.

Susan loves **babies**.

LET'S CHECK

A 명사의 성격이 다른 하나를 고르세요.

0	box	(tiger)	chair	truck
1	dog	bear	zoo	duck
2	doctor	hospital	student	teacher
3	city	park	artist	museum
4	kite	map	computer	eagle
5	ball	school	hat	basket
6	snake	scientist	bee	elephant
7	koala	rabbit	forest	panda

B 주어진 명사의 복수형을 쓰세요.

0	desk	_desks_	10	potato	_____
1	shirt	_____	11	tomato	_____
2	egg	_____	12	hero	_____
3	friend	_____	13	piano	_____
4	rose	_____	14	photo	_____
5	bus	_____	15	leaf	_____
6	dress	_____	16	wife	_____
7	bench	_____	17	shelf	_____
8	brush	_____	18	city	_____
9	fox	_____	19	monkey	_____

WORDS   A hospital 병원   kite 연   map 지도   eagle 독수리   hat 모자   basket 바구니   bee 벌   forest 숲   B brush 붓; 솔   fox 여우   hero 영웅   leaf 잎   shelf 선반

❷ 불규칙 변화

man → **men**	foot → **feet**	mouse → **mice**	fish → **fish**
woman → **women**	tooth → **teeth**	ox → **oxen**	sheep → **sheep**
person → **people**	goose → **geese**	child → **children**	deer → **deer**

NOTE fish, sheep, deer는 단수형과 복수형이 같으므로 주의한다.

The farmer has a **sheep.** [○]

The farmer has three **sheep.** [○]

The farmer has three **sheeps.** [×]

4 항상 복수형으로 쓰는 명사

두 개가 모여 한 쌍을 이루는 경우에는 복수형을 쓴다.

glasses	scissors	gloves	socks
pants	jeans	shorts	shoes

(+PLUS) 위 명사들은 주로 '한 쌍의'란 의미의 a pair of와 함께 쓰인다.

a pair of scissors 가위 한 개

two pairs of socks 양말 두 켤레

three pairs of jeans 청바지 세 벌

Your **jean** is really nice. [×]

Your **jeans** are really nice. [○]

I want to buy **one pant.** [×]

I want to buy **a pair of pants.** [○]

LET'S CHECK

C 보기에서 알맞은 말을 골라 복수형을 써서 빈칸을 완성하세요. (단, 한 번씩만 쓸 것)

보기	man	~~woman~~	tooth	child	mouse	foot	ox	deer
	fish	goose	glove	person	sheep	jean	shoe	

0

three <u>women</u>

1

three _____

2

five _____

3

two _____

4

two _____

5

five _____

6

two _____

7

two _____

8

three _____

9

three _____

10

two _____

11

three _____

12

a pair of _____

13

a pair of _____

14

a pair of _____

WORDS   **C** tooth 이, 치아   mouse 쥐, 생쥐   foot 발   ox 황소   deer 사슴   goose 거위   sheep 양   jeans 청바지

LET'S PRACTICE

A 주어진 명사의 복수형을 쓰세요.

0   one hat, two _____hats_____

1   one class, two _____

2   one tooth, two _____

3   a flower, many _____

4   one watch, five _____

5   one box, ten _____

6   one potato, five _____

7   one wolf, six _____

8   a library, many _____

9   a toy, three _____

10 one orange, two _____

11 a child, four _____

12 one man, five _____

13 one goose, three _____

14 a photo, many _____

15 one thief, two _____

16 one foot, two _____

17 a hero, many _____

18 a deer, five _____

19 one ox, two _____

B ( ) 안에서 알맞은 말을 고르세요.

0   Jane has two (balloon, (balloons)).

1   There is a (mouse, mice) in the hole.

2   Look! There is a (fly, flies) in the web.

3   Owls have big (eye, eyes).

4   (Rose, Roses) are beautiful flowers.

5   (Sheep, Sheeps) eat grass.

6   They are (musician, musicians).

7   She is a good (teacher, teachers).

8   Nora eats (apple, an apple) every morning.

9   Joe needs a new (shirt, shirts) and a pair of (pant, pants).

WORDS   A watch 시계   wolf 늑대   thief 도둑   B balloon 풍선   hole 구멍   fly 파리   web 거미줄   owl 올빼미, 부엉이   grass 풀, 잔디
musician 음악가

C 그림을 보고 보기에서 알맞은 말을 골라 적절한 형태로 바꾸어 문장을 완성하세요.

0  1  2 3

| 보기 | ~~cookie~~ | month | puppy | tooth |

0 These _____cookies_____ are delicious.

1 They are my _____.

2 The baby has two _____.

3 There are twelve _____ in a year.

D 밑줄 친 부분을 바르게 고치세요.

0 A triangle has three <u>side</u>. → *sides*

1 There are many <u>star</u> in the sky. →

2 We need two <u>potatos</u>. →

3 <u>Leafs</u> turn red and yellow in fall. →

4 I need <u>a scissor</u>. →

5 Mike eats two <u>sandwich</u> for lunch. →

6 Mr. Kim has two <u>childs</u>. →

7 <u>Fishes</u> live in water. →

8 Doctors help sick <u>peoples</u>. →

9 Two <u>womans</u> are on the sofa. →

WORDS   C puppy 강아지 delicious 맛있는   D triangle 삼각형 side 면, (도형의) 변 fall 가을 sick 아픈

셀 수 없는 명사
Uncountable Nouns

1 셀 수 없는 명사

물(water), 공기(air)처럼 일정한 형태가 없거나 입자가 너무 작아서 '하나, 둘…' 셀 수 없는 명사이다. 셀 수 없는 명사는 다음과 같은 종류가 있다.

셀 수 없는 물질	water, milk, tea, bread, cheese, meat, gold, soap, sugar, salt, rice, paper, air, gas …
추상적인 개념	love, peace, friendship, happiness, time, advice …
고유 명사	Alice, Seoul, Canada, April, Christmas …
기타 (총칭, 자연현상, 언어, 학과목, 운동)	money, mail, food, furniture, work, homework, rain, snow, English, math, tennis …

(+PLUS) 고유 명사는 세상에 하나뿐인 특정한 사람, 사물, 장소 등의 이름으로 항상 대문자로 시작한다.

My name is **Amy.**　　　　　　　My sister lives in **France.**

2 셀 수 없는 명사의 특징

'하나, 둘…' 셀 수 없으므로 a/an을 붙일 수 없고 항상 단수형으로 쓴다.

A love is great. [×]

Love is great. [○]

Plants need **waters.** [×]

Plants need **water.** [○]

3 셀 수 없는 명사의 수량 표현

셀 수 없는 물질은 그것을 담는 용기나 모양을 단위로 수를 센다. 복수형을 나타낼 때는 단위 명사에 -(e)s를 붙인다.

• **a glass of** water/milk/juice	• **a piece[sheet] of** paper
• **a cup of** coffee/tea	• **a bar of** soap/chocolate
• **a bottle of** water/milk/juice/wine	• **a loaf of** bread
• **a bowl of** rice/soup/cereal	• **a slice[piece] of** bread/pizza/cheese
• **a can of** Coke/corn	• **a box of** chocolate/candy/cereal

I want **a cup of tea.**

He has **two pieces of paper.**

LET'S CHECK

A 셀 수 없는 명사를 모두 고르세요.

(milk)	cat	sugar	friend	rice
butter	spoon	air	bus	rain
house	soccer	flower	bread	paper
knife	eraser	money	English	toy
orange	meat	math	photo	friendship

B 그림을 보고 빈칸에 알맞은 말을 쓰세요.

0

a ___cup___ of tea

1

a _____ of soap

2

a _____ of chocolate

3

a _____ of Coke

4

a _____ of water

5

a _____ of bread

6

a _____ of milk

7

a _____ of paper

8

a _____ of soup

9

a _____ of bread

10

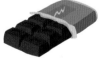

a _____ of chocolate

11

a _____ of cheese

WORDS   A rice 쌀 air 공기 eraser 지우개 math 수학 friendship 우정   B soap 비누

LET'S PRACTICE

A 밑줄 친 명사가 셀 수 있는 명사이면 C, 셀 수 없는 명사이면 U를 쓰세요.

0   He likes Korean pop <u>songs</u>.

1   I listen to <u>music</u> on the bus.

2   We need two <u>chairs</u>.

3   She has some old <u>furniture</u>.

4   I have a <u>coin</u> in my pocket.

5   They need some <u>money</u>.

6   I like Chinese <u>food</u>.

7   Monkeys like <u>bananas</u>.

8   Peter enjoys his <u>work</u>.

9   <u>Science</u> is difficult for me.

C

B 그림을 보고 보기에서 알맞은 말을 골라 ( ) 안의 말과 함께 써서 수량을 나타내세요. (단, 한 번씩만 쓸 것)

0    1    2    3

보기	~~bottle~~	glass	sheet	slice

0   _____a bottle of milk_____   (milk)

1   _____   (paper)

2   _____   (juice)

3   _____   (cheese)

WORDS   A furniture 가구   coin 동전   difficult 어려운   B sheet 한 장

C

( ) 안에서 알맞은 말을 고르세요.

0   ((Gold), A gold) is expensive.

1   I need some (salt, salts).

2   They play (soccer, a soccer) after school.

3   There is (snow, snows) on the roof.

4   People want (peace, a peace) in the world.

5   Bees collect (honey, honeys).

6   They speak (Korean, a Korean).

7   I eat a (bowl, loaf) of cereal for breakfast.

8   Judy wants (two pieces of cake, two pieces of cakes).

9   Sam drinks (two coffees, two cups of coffee) a day.

D

밑줄 친 부분을 바르게 고치세요.

0   Sue drinks <u>teas</u> after meals.   →   tea

1   <u>A time</u> is money.   →

2   There is some <u>foods</u> in the refrigerator.   →

3   Susan doesn't eat <u>a meat</u>.   →

4   I do my <u>homeworks</u> in the evening.   →

5   They live in <u>a New York</u>.   →

6   I'm thirsty. I want <u>a glass water</u>.   →

7   Two <u>bowls of soups</u> are on the table.   →

8   I need a pen and <u>papers</u>.   →

9   We have three <u>loafs of bread</u>.   →

WORDS   C gold 금 expensive 비싼 salt 소금 peace 평화 collect 모으다, 수집하다   D meal 식사 refrigerator 냉장고 thirsty 목마른

STEP 1

빈칸 완성 보기에서 알맞은 말을 골라 적절한 형태로 바꾸어 문장을 완성하세요.

보기	nurse	peach	scarf	soldier	tooth

1 내 사촌은 간호사이다.

→ My cousin is a   .

2 그들은 군인이다.

→ They are   .

3 그녀의 치아는 하얗다.

→ Her   are white.

4 이 스카프들은 멋지다.

→ These   are nice.

5 복숭아 다섯 개가 바구니에 있다.

→ There are five   in the basket.

STEP 2

어구 배열 우리말과 일치하도록 ( ) 안의 말을 알맞게 배열하세요.

6 나에게 피자 두 조각이 있다. (have, pieces, pizza, of, two, I)

→ _____

7 우리는 오늘 숙제가 많다. (homework, we, a lot of, have, today)

→ _____

8 그는 유명한 가수이다. (is, famous, he, a, singer)

→ _____

9 그들은 쌍둥이 자매이다. (are, sisters, they, twin)

→ _____

10 나는 숟가락과 젓가락이 필요하다. (need, a, chopsticks, I, and, spoon)

→ _____

STEP 3

영작하기 (   ) 안의 말을 이용하여 우리말을 영어로 옮기세요.

11 그녀는 토마토와 고구마를 기른다. (tomato, sweet potato)

→ She grows _____ and _____.

12 그들은 세 명의 자녀가 있다. (child)

→ They have _____.

13 그들은 좋은 이웃이다. (good, neighbor)

→ They are _____.

14 Ted는 두꺼운 안경을 쓴다. (thick, glass)

→ Ted wears _____.

15 나에게 펜 두 개와 종이 세 장이 있다. (pen, sheet, paper)

→ I have _____ and _____.

16 나에게 설탕이 좀 있다. (some, sugar)

→ I have _____.

17 David는 4개 국어를 말한다. (language)

→ David speaks _____.

18 그는 물 다섯 병이 필요하다. (bottle, water)

→ He needs _____.

19 우리는 포크와 칼이 더 필요하다. (fork, knife)

→ We need more _____ and _____.

20 그는 일주일에 5일을 일한다. (day)

→ He works _____ a week.

1 명사의 성격이 나머지 넷과 다른 것은?

① box ② tree ③ chair

④ house ⑤ paper

[2-3] 빈칸에 'a'가 들어갈 수 없는 것을 고르시오.

2 ① She is _____ doctor.

② Mr. Kim has _____ son.

③ _____ bird is in the sky.

④ He is from _____ Canada.

⑤ Seoul is _____ city in Korea.

3 ① We have _____ dog.

② They are _____ friends.

③ James drives _____ bus.

④ That is _____ tall building.

⑤ I need _____ new cellphone.

[4-5] 명사의 단수형과 복수형이 잘못 연결된 것을 고르시오.

4 ① fox – foxes

② bus – buses

③ dish – dishes

④ class – classes

⑤ tomato – tomatos

5 ① toy – toys

② eye – eyes

③ knife – knives

④ radio – radios

⑤ sheep – sheeps

서술형

6 짝지어진 단어의 관계가 일치하도록 빈칸에 알맞은 말을 쓰시오.

rose : roses = _____ : puppies

man : men = mouse : _____

7 밑줄 친 부분이 잘못된 것은?

① A spider has eight legs.

② The truck has six wheels.

③ She needs four potatoes.

④ Two thiefs are in the house.

⑤ Two dictionaries are on the desk.

8 다음 중 잘못된 표현은?

① a bar of soap

② a sheet of paper

③ two pieces of cake

④ two slices of cheeses

⑤ eight glasses of water

9 빈칸에 들어갈 말로 알맞지 <u>않은</u> 것은?

> He has three _____.

① cats ② fish ③ breads
④ geese ⑤ children

10 밑줄 친 ①~⑤ 중 어법상 어색한 것은?

> Julie has <u>a banana</u>, <u>a bowl</u> of <u>cereal</u>,
>   ①   ②   ③
> and <u>two glass</u> of <u>orange juice</u> for
>   ④   ⑤
> breakfast.

[11-12] 밑줄 친 부분이 옳은 것을 고르시오.

11 ① Look at these <u>scarfs</u>.
② John wears <u>a glasses</u>.
③ <u>Deer</u> live in the woods.
④ These <u>peachs</u> are sweet.
⑤ Soda is bad for your <u>tooths</u>.

12 ① We need <u>a salt</u>.
② I like <u>rock musics</u>.
③ They speak <u>an English</u>.
④ <u>A math</u> is difficult for me.
⑤ I need <u>an egg and butter</u>.

서술형

[13-14] ( ) 안의 말을 이용하여 문장을 완성하시오.

13

> Two _____ are in the living room.
> (piano)

14

> I have some _____ in my pocket.
> (money)

서술형

[15-17] 우리말과 일치하도록 ( ) 안의 말을 이용하여
문장을 완성하시오.

15

> 그의 손과 발은 크다. (hand, foot)

→ He has big _____ and
_____.

16

> 중국과 인도는 아시아에 있는 나라이다. (country)

→ China and India are _____
in Asia.

17

> 나에게 빵 두 덩어리가 있다. (loaf, bread)

→ I have two _____.

CHAPTER
02
Articles
관사

LET'S LOOK

a tree

an umbrella

the door

관사는 명사 앞에 쓰여 그 명사가 막연한 하나인지 또는 특정한 것인지를 알려주는 말이다. 관사에는 **부정관사 a/an**과 **정관사 the** 두 가지 형태가 있다.

03 부정관사 A/An
The Indefinite Articles *A/An*

1 부정관사 a/an

❶ 셀 수 있는 명사의 단수형 앞에 써서 정해지지 않은 사람이나 사물을 나타낸다.

There is **a boy** at the door.

I have **an apple**.

> **NOTE** '하나의'라는 의미를 나타내므로 복수명사와 셀 수 없는 명사 앞에는 a/an을 쓰지 않는다.
> *a balls* [×]   *an eggs* [×]   *a milk* [×]   *an air* [×]

❷ 뒤에 오는 명사의 첫 소리가 자음이면 a, 모음이면 an을 쓴다.

a + 자음	**a d**og	**a g**irl	**a t**rain	**a w**eek	**a y**ear
an + 모음	**an a**ctor	**an e**lephant	**an i**gloo	**an o**range	**an u**mbrella

> **NOTE** 1. h로 시작하는 명사는 첫 소리가 자음 [h]이면 a를 쓰고 모음 [a]이면 an을 쓴다.
> **a** house   **a** hotel   **an** hour   **an** honor
>
> 2. u로 시작하는 명사는 첫 소리가 반자음 [j]이면 a, 모음 [ʌ]이면 an을 쓴다.
> **a** uniform   **a** university   **an** uncle   **an** umbrella
>
> 3. w, y로 시작하는 명사 앞에는 a를 쓴다.
> **a** week   **a** window   **a** year   **a** yo-yo

❸ 명사 앞에 형용사가 있는 경우에는 형용사가 모음으로 시작하면 an을 쓴다.

It is **an old** house.

He is **an honest** man.

2 부정관사 a/an의 의미

특정하지 않은 사람 또는 사물 (같은 종류 중 어떤 하나를 가리킴)	She is **a** teacher. 그녀는 선생님 (한 분)이다. It is **a** balloon. 그것은 풍선 (하나)이다. I need **an** umbrella. 나는 우산이 (하나) 필요하다. (이 경우, 'one'보다 가벼운 의미로 보통은 '하나의'로 해석하지 않는다.)
하나 (= one)	**A** day has 24 hours. 하루는 24시간이다.
~마다, 매 ~ (= per)	They play soccer once **a** week. 그들은 일주일에 한 번 축구를 한다.
종족 전체	**A** cow is an animal. (= Cows are animals.) 소는 동물이다.

LET'S CHECK

A 빈칸에 a, an 중 알맞은 것을 쓰세요.

0	___a___ chair	10	_____ bike
1	_____ airplane	11	_____ idea
2	_____ pencil	12	_____ toy
3	_____ orange	13	_____ onion
4	_____ doctor	14	_____ hour
5	_____ uniform	15	_____ map
6	_____ elephant	16	_____ uncle
7	_____ woman	17	_____ hotel
8	_____ zebra	18	_____ artist
9	_____ octopus	19	_____ umbrella

B 우리말과 일치하도록 빈칸에 a, an을 쓰세요.

0	유명한 배우	→	___a___ famous actor
1	미국인 남성	→	_____ American man
2	좋은 생각	→	_____ good idea
3	비싼 자동차	→	_____ expensive car
4	재미있는 책	→	_____ interesting book
5	노란색 우비	→	_____ yellow raincoat
6	이탈리아 식당	→	_____ Italian restaurant
7	높은 산	→	_____ high mountain
8	일년에 한 번	→	once _____ year
9	일주일에 두 번	→	twice _____ week

WORDS   A airplane 비행기   uniform 교복   zebra 얼룩말   octopus 문어   onion 양파   umbrella 우산   B actor 배우
interesting 재미있는   mountain 산

LET'S PRACTICE

A ( ) 안에서 알맞은 말을 고르세요. (X는 필요 없음을 뜻함)

0 ((a,) an, X) girl

1 (a, an, X) water

2 (a, an, X) lion

3 (a, an, X) album

4 (a, an, X) computers

5 (a, an, X) child

6 (a, an, X) salt

7 (a, an, X) hat

8 (a, an, X) office

9 (a, an, X) day

10 (a, an, X) books

11 (a, an, X) student

12 (a, an, X) ant

13 (a, an, X) butter

14 (a, an, X) igloo

15 (a, an, X) university

16 (a, an, X) pineapple

17 (a, an, X) ears

18 (a, an, X) island

19 (a, an, X) window

B 빈칸에 a, an 중 알맞은 것을 쓰고, 필요 없는 경우에는 X를 쓰세요.

0 I have _____a_____ dog in my house.

1 She eats _____ bread for breakfast.

2 I have _____ pencil and _____ eraser.

3 My father is _____ engineer.

4 Brian is _____ honest boy.

5 There is _____ milk in the bottle.

6 My sister is _____ university student.

7 _____ elephant has _____ big ears.

8 New York is _____ interesting city.

9 I visit my grandparents once _____ month.

WORDS A album 앨범 office 사무실 university 대학 island 섬 B engineer 기사, 엔지니어 honest 정직한 visit 방문하다

C 그림을 보고 보기에서 알맞은 말을 골라 a, an과 함께 써서 문장을 완성하세요.

0  1  2  3

| 보기 | astronaut | ~~dentist~~ | English teacher | photographer |

0 Jane is _____ a dentist _____.

1 Mike is _____.

2 Sara is _____.

3 John is _____.

D 밑줄 친 부분이 맞으면 O를 쓰고, 틀리면 바르게 고치세요.

0 I need <u>an</u> map. → a

1 Bali is <u>an</u> island. →

2 They live in <u>an</u> house. →

3 Mary wears <u>a</u> uniform. →

4 I need <u>a</u> egg, flour, and some sugar. →

5 My brother has <u>a</u> hamster. →

6 I read a <u>books</u> every day. →

7 He drinks <u>an orange juice</u> every morning. →

8 I have <u>a</u> uncle. His name is Bob. →

9 They meet together once <u>a</u> week. →

WORDS C astronaut 우주 비행사 dentist 치과 의사 photographer 사진작가, 사진사 D flour 밀가루 hamster 햄스터 together 함께

04 정관사 The

The Definite Article *The*

1 정관사 the

정해져 있는 특정한 사람이나 사물을 나타낼 때 쓴다. '그'라는 의미를 나타내므로 셀 수 있는 명사의 단수와 복수, 셀 수 없는 명사 앞에 모두 쓰일 수 있다.

❶ 앞에서 이미 언급된 것

He has *a dog*. **The** dog is black.

❷ 서로 알고 있는 것

I'm cold. Close **the** door, please.

A: Where is Tony? B: He is in **the** kitchen.

❸ 세상에서 유일한 것

the sun	**the** moon	**the** Earth	**the** sky

❹ 연주하는 악기 앞

play **the** piano	play **the** guitar	play **the** violin	play **the** flute

> ✏ NOTE 관용적으로 the를 쓰는 경우
>
> | go to the doctor 병원에 가다 | go to the dentist 치과에 가다 |
> |---|---|
> | go to the movies 영화 보러 가다 | listen to the radio 라디오를 듣다 |
> | on the Internet 인터넷에서 | |

2 관사를 쓰지 않는 경우

다음과 같은 경우에는 명사 앞에 관사(a/an, the)를 쓰지 않는다.

식사 이름 앞	breakfast, lunch, dinner …
운동 이름 앞	basketball, soccer, tennis, golf …
by + 교통수단	by bus 버스로, by taxi 택시로, by car 차로, by train 기차로
과목, 언어 앞	math, science, English, Chinese …
장소가 본래 목적을 의미할 때	go to school 등교하다, go to church 예배 보러 가다, go to bed 잠자리에 들다

They play **basketball** after **lunch**.

Mike goes to **school** by **bus**.

She speaks **Chinese** well.

LET'S CHECK

A ( ) 안에서 알맞은 말을 고르세요.

0 (A, (The)) Earth is round.

1 A butterfly is (an, the) insect.

2 Please turn off (a, the) TV.

3 My parents are in (a, the) garden.

4 I have three meals (a, the) day.

5 (A, The) sky is nice and clear.

6 Jessie drives a car. (A, The) car is blue.

7 Bill has (a, the) dog and two cats.

8 The little boy plays (a, the) guitar very well.

9 There is (a, the) letter for you.

B 우리말과 일치하도록 빈칸에 the, X 중 알맞은 것을 쓰세요. (X는 필요 없음을 뜻함)

0	저녁 식사를 하다	→	have ____X____ dinner
1	병원에 가다	→	go to _____ doctor
2	영어를 말하다	→	speak _____ English
3	수학을 공부하다	→	study _____ math
4	영화 보러 가다	→	go to _____ movies
5	농구를 하다	→	play _____ basketball
6	라디오를 듣다	→	listen to _____ radio
7	기차로 여행하다	→	travel by _____ train
8	인터넷에서 옷을 사다	→	buy clothes on _____ Internet
9	등교하다	→	go to _____ school

WORDS   A butterfly 나비 insect 곤충 turn off 끄다 guitar 기타 letter 편지   B clothes 옷

LET'S PRACTICE

A 빈칸에 들어갈 말로 알맞은 것을 고르세요.

0 (1) _____ rose is a flower.   ☑ A   ☐ The

   (2) _____ rose is yellow.   ☐ A   ☑ The

1 (1) Is there _____ bathroom around here?   ☐ a   ☐ the

   (2) Tom is in _____ bathroom.   ☐ a   ☐ the

2 (1) _____ box is heavy.   ☐ A   ☐ The

   (2) _____ box has six sides.   ☐ A   ☐ The

3 (1) _____ coat is very expensive.   ☐ A   ☐ The

   (2) I want _____ new coat.   ☐ a   ☐ the

4 (1) I have _____ idea.   ☐ an   ☐ the

   (2) I like _____ idea.   ☐ an   ☐ the

B 빈칸에 the, X 중 알맞은 것을 쓰세요. (X는 필요 없음을 뜻함)

0 In summer, ___the___ sun is very hot.

1 Let's go there by _____ taxi.

2 Kevin has _____ breakfast at 7:00 a.m.

3 _____ woman is my aunt.

4 He practices _____ violin every day.

5 They learn _____ Chinese.

6 Nancy goes to _____ bed at 10:00 p.m.

7 There are dark clouds in _____ sky.

8 My favorite subject is _____ music.

9 I have a test tomorrow. _____ test is very important.

WORDS   A coat 외투, 코트   B aunt 숙모   practice 연습하다   subject 과목   important 중요한

C 그림을 보고 보기에서 알맞은 말을 골라 문장을 완성하세요. (필요한 경우 the를 쓸 것)

0  1  2  3

| 보기 | salt | ~~moon~~ | lunch | badminton |

0 _____The moon_____ is bright tonight.

1 They play _____ together.

2 Pass me _____, please.

3 Jim has a sandwich for _____.

D 밑줄 친 부분이 맞으면 O를 쓰고, 틀리면 바르게 고치세요.

0 Rome is <u>a city</u>. →   *O*

1 <u>A</u> boy is my brother. →

2 He comes home <u>by a car</u>. →

3 <u>Sun</u> is above my head. →

4 I have a pen. <u>The pen</u> is blue. →

5 Jack has <u>a</u> nice watch. →

6 I don't like <u>the math</u>. →

7 He plays <u>a golf</u> once a month. →

8 <u>The bike</u> is new. →

9 Your shirt is in <u>the washing machine</u>. →

WORDS　C badminton 배드민턴　bright 밝은　D above ~ 위에　washing machine 세탁기

STEP 1

빈칸 완성 보기에서 알맞은 말을 골라 a, an, the와 함께 써서 문장을 완성하세요.

| 보기 | earring | hour | question | sky | water |

1 당신에게 질문이 하나 있어요.

→ I have _____ _____ for you.

2 한 시간은 60분이다.

→ _____ _____ has sixty minutes.

3 그는 귀걸이를 하나 착용한다.

→ He wears _____ _____ .

4 컵 안의 물은 따뜻하다.

→ _____ _____ in the cup is warm.

5 하늘 좀 봐.

→ Look at _____ _____ .

STEP 2

어구 배열 우리말과 일치하도록 (   ) 안의 말을 알맞게 배열하세요.

6 나에게 우산이 하나 있다. (umbrella, I, an, have)

→ _____

7 타조는 큰 새이다. (ostrich, a, is, bird, an, large)

→ _____

8 그 남자는 작가이다. (man, is, a, the, writer)

→ _____

9 나의 형은 드럼을 친다. (my, the, brother, drums, plays)

→ _____

10 우리는 정오에 점심을 먹는다. (eat, we, at noon, lunch)

→ _____

영작하기 ( ) 안의 말을 이용하여 우리말을 영어로 옮기세요.

11 그것은 오래된 건물이다. (it, is, old building)

→ _____

12 문어는 다리가 8개이다. (octopus, has, eight, leg)

→ _____

13 Ann은 고등학생이다. (Ann, is, high school student)

→ _____

14 Mike는 노란색 차를 운전한다. (Mike, drives, yellow car)

→ _____

15 나는 그 소녀를 매일 본다. (I, see, girl, every day)

→ _____

16 그는 1년에 두 번 한국을 방문한다. (he, visits, Korea, twice, year)

→ _____

17 그 소년은 새 자전거를 원한다. (boy, wants, new bike)

→ _____

18 아빠는 거실에서 TV를 보신다. (Dad, watches, TV, in, living room)

→ _____

19 그는 한국어와 일본어를 한다. (he, speaks, Korean, Japanese)

→ _____

20 사람들은 배를 타고 그 섬에 간다. (people, go to the island, by, ship)

→ _____

REVIEW TEST
CHAPTER 02

[1-2] 빈칸에 들어갈 말로 알맞지 <u>않은</u> 것을 고르시오.

1

> She has a _____.

① cat　　② book　　③ house

④ pencil　　⑤ umbrella

2

> This is an _____.

① apple　　② orange　　③ onion

④ watch　　⑤ elephant

서술형

3 빈칸에 a 또는 an을 넣어 문장을 완성하시오.

> · It is _____ interesting book.
> · Jessie wears _____ uniform.

4 밑줄 친 부분이 <u>잘못된</u> 것은?

① It is <u>an old book</u>.

② Jim is <u>a honest boy</u>.

③ He is <u>a famous actor</u>.

④ It is <u>an easy question</u>.

⑤ Judy is <u>an American girl</u>.

5 빈칸에 들어갈 말이 순서대로 바르게 짝지어진 것은?

> They live in _____ apartment.
> _____ apartment building is on
> 5th Street.

① a – An　　② an – A

③ a – The　　④ an – The

⑤ the – The

서술형

[6-8] 보기에서 알맞은 말을 골라 문장을 완성하시오.

> | 보기 | a　　an　　the |
> |---|---|

6

> A snake is _____ animal.

7

> _____ sun rises in the east.

8

> Apples are 10 dollars _____ kilo.

서술형

9 빈칸에 공통으로 들어갈 말을 쓰시오.

> · The buses go to _____ airport.
> · I clean _____ house every day.
> · There is a helicopter in _____ sky.

10 밑줄 친 ①~⑤중 어법상 어색한 것은?

> Mr. Kim has <u>two children</u> — <u>a boy</u> and
>   ①   ②
> <u>a girl</u>. <u>A boy</u> is five, and <u>the girl</u> is ten.
> ③   ④   ⑤

11 빈칸에 들어갈 관사가 나머지 넷과 다른 것은?

> ① _____ shoes are new.
> ② We live on _____ Earth.
> ③ _____ day has 24 hours.
> ④ Turn on _____ light, please.
> ⑤ Mom and Dad are in _____ kitchen.

12 밑줄 친 부분이 옳은 것은?

> ① I <u>eat a lunch</u> at 12:30.
> ② We <u>study math</u> together.
> ③ The girls <u>speak a Chinese</u>.
> ④ They <u>play the tennis</u> every day.
> ⑤ George <u>goes to a bed</u> before 10.

서술형

13 어법상 <u>틀린</u> 부분을 찾아 바르게 고치시오.

> I exercise for a hour every day.

_____ → _____

서술형

[14-17] 우리말과 일치하도록 ( ) 안의 말을 이용하여 문장을 완성하시오.

14
> 나는 햄버거 한 개와 감자튀김을 원한다.
> (hamburger, French fries)

→ I want _____ and _____ .

15
> 우리는 일년에 두 번 휴가를 떠난다. (twice, year)

→ We go on vacation _____ .

16
> 그녀는 오케스트라에서 첼로를 연주한다. (cello)

→ She plays _____ in the orchestra.

17
> 내 친구들과 나는 버스로 학교에 간다. (by, bus)

→ My friends and I go to school _____ .

CHAPTER
03

Pronouns
대명사

LET'S LOOK

I

she

they

대명사는 명사를 대신해서 쓰는 말이다. 대명사는 사람이나 사물의 이름을 대신해서 부르는 **인칭대명사**와 가까이 있거나 멀리 있는 대상을 가리키는 **지시대명사** 등이 있다.

05 인칭대명사
Personal Pronouns

1 대명사

대명사는 명사를 대신해서 쓰는 말이다. 주로 명사의 반복을 피하기 위해 쓴다.

Mr. Wilson is a doctor. **He** helps sick people.
                             = Mr. Wilson

2 인칭대명사

❶ 인칭대명사는 사람 또는 사물의 이름을 '나, 너, 그, 그것' 등으로 대신해서 나타내는 말이다.

my sister → **she**   the bag → **it**   the boys → **they**   Mike and I → **we**

❷ 인칭대명사는 수에 따라 단수와 복수로 나뉘고, 인칭에 따라 1인칭(나/우리), 2인칭(너/너희들), 3인칭(그/그녀/그것/그들)으로 구분한다.

3 주격, 목적격 인칭대명사

수	인칭	주격(~는, ~가)	목적격(~을/를)
	1인칭	I 나는	me 나를
단수	2인칭	you 너는	you 너를
	3인칭	he/she/it 그는/그녀는/그것은	him/her/it 그를/그녀를/그것을
	1인칭	we 우리는	us 우리를
복수	2인칭	you 너희들은	you 너희들을
	3인칭	they 그(것)들은	them 그(것)들을

❶ 주격은 '~는, ~가'를 의미하며 문장에서 주어 역할을 한다.

I know Clair. **She** is my classmate.

Madrid is a city. **It** is in Spain.

❷ 목적격은 '~을/를'을 의미하며 동사와 전치사 뒤에서 목적어 역할을 한다.

My uncle lives in Busan. I *visit* **him** every summer.

I like her songs. I listen *to* **them** every day.

LET'S CHECK

A 밑줄 친 말을 주격 대명사로 바꿔 쓰세요.

0 <u>My aunt</u> is a nurse. → She

1 <u>Mr. Brown</u> is from London. →

2 <u>Bill and Susie</u> go to school together. →

3 <u>You and I</u> are good friends. →

4 <u>You and Jinho</u> are in the same class. →

5 <u>Mr. and Mrs. White</u> have a daughter. →

6 <u>The building</u> is our school. →

7 <u>The mountains</u> are so high. →

8 <u>The men</u> are hockey players. →

9 <u>Cathy, Dave, and I</u> are tall. →

B 밑줄 친 말을 가리키는 목적격 대명사를 쓰세요.

0 I like <u>apples</u>. I eat ____them____ every day.

1 Where is <u>my ruler</u>? I need _____ right now.

2 <u>I</u> love my parents. They love _____, too.

3 When is <u>your birthday</u>? I don't remember _____.

4 <u>Mrs. Parker</u> is very kind. Everybody likes _____.

5 <u>My sister</u> lives in Japan. I miss _____ very much.

6 <u>My grandparents</u> live with me. I love _____.

7 <u>We</u> like our teacher. He is kind to _____.

8 Who is <u>that boy</u>? I don't know _____.

9 <u>The old man</u> has a dog. It follows _____ everywhere.

WORDS A nurse 간호사 daughter 딸 B ruler 자 remember 기억하다 miss 그리워하다 follow 따라가다

4 소유격 인칭대명사, 소유대명사

수	인칭	소유격(~의)	소유대명사(~의 것)
단수	1인칭	my 나의	mine 나의 것
	2인칭	your 너의	yours 너의 것
	3인칭	his/her/its 그의/그녀의/그것의	his/hers/– 그의 것/그녀의 것/–
복수	1인칭	our 우리의	ours 우리의 것
	2인칭	your 너희들의	yours 너희들의 것
	3인칭	their 그(것)들의	theirs 그(것)들의 것

❶ 소유격은 '~의'를 의미하며 뒤에 반드시 명사가 온다.

She is **my** *sister*. **Her** *name* is Sally.

I have a pen. **Its** *color* is red.

❷ 소유대명사는 '~의 것'을 의미한다. 소유대명사는 「소유격 + 명사」를 대신하므로 뒤에 명사가 오지 않는다.

The bag is <u>mine</u>.
= my bag

My shoes are blue. <u>**Yours**</u> are brown.
= Your shoes

5 명사의 소유격

❶ 명사의 소유격은 「명사 + 's」로 나타낸다.

Jane's room

the **monkey's** tail

❷ -s로 끝나는 복수명사의 소유격은 아포스트로피(')만 붙인다. -s로 끝나지 않는 복수명사는 's를 붙인다.

the **girls'** names

the **children's** toys

❸ 무생물의 소유격은 「of + 명사」로 나타낸다.

the roof **of the house**

the color **of the coat**

LET'S CHECK

C   빈칸에 알맞은 소유격 대명사와 소유대명사를 쓰세요.

0   I have a book.   (1) It is _____my_____ book.

                                      (2) The book is _____mine_____.

1   You have a bag.   (1) It is _____ bag.

                                      (2) The bag is _____.

2   She has an umbrella.   (1) It is _____ umbrella.

                                      (2) The umbrella is _____.

3   We have a dog.   (1) It is _____ dog.

                                      (2) The dog is _____.

4   They have a house.   (1) It is _____ house.

                                      (2) The house is _____.

D   ( ) 안에서 알맞은 말을 고르세요.

0   They are (my, mine) pencils.

1   The red car is (their, theirs).

2   (Your, Yours) hair is long. (My, Mine) is short.

3   These letters are (you, yours).

4   Nora washes (her, hers) hair every day.

5   Their class is boring. (Our, Ours) is interesting.

6   France is famous for (it, its) wine.

7   These are (my cat's toys, the toys of my cat).

8   This is (Uncle Jack's house, the house of Uncle Jack).

9   (The truck's wheels, The wheels of the truck) are big.

WORDS   D boring 지루한   be famous for ~로 유명하다   wheel 바퀴

LET'S PRACTICE

A 다음 표를 완성하세요.

수	인칭	주격	목적격	소유격	소유대명사
단수	1인칭	(1)	me	(2)	mine
	2인칭	you	(3)	(4)	yours
	3인칭	he	(5)	his	(6)
		she	her	(7)	(8)
		it	(9)	(10)	–
복수	1인칭	(11)	us	(12)	(13)
	2인칭	you	(14)	(15)	yours
	3인칭	they	(16)	their	(17)

B ( ) 안에서 알맞은 말을 고르세요.

0 Alex is my friend. I know (he, (him)) very well.

1 I like peaches. My mom often buys (it, them) for me.

2 The boys ride (his, their) bikes to school.

3 Turn down the radio. (It, Its) is too loud.

4 I have a cousin. (He, His) name is Steve.

5 I have a sister. (She, Her) is 19 years old.

6 Jessica, I need (you, your) help.

7 (I, My) am Kim Yuna.

8 The puppies are (us, ours).

9 My father and (I, me) go hiking on Sundays.

WORDS   B often 종종, 자주   ride 타다   turn down (소리를) 낮추다, 줄이다   loud 큰, 시끄러운   cousin 사촌   go hiking 하이킹을 가다

C 그림을 보고 보기에서 알맞은 말을 골라 문장을 완성하세요.

0	1	2	3

보기	her	~~it~~	mine	them

0   I have a cat. _____It_____ has three kittens.

1   Lucy's umbrella is red. _____ is yellow.

2   My grandparents live in the country. I visit _____ every month.

3   _____ necklace looks expensive.

D ( ) 안의 말을 적절한 형태로 바꾸어 빈칸에 쓰세요.

0   Daniel likes _____his_____ job. (he)

1   This is my new computer. _____ is very fast. (it)

2   I know Megan and _____ sisters. (she)

3   He has two children. I know _____. (they)

4   Spring is _____ favorite season. (I)

5   Goodbye. See _____ tomorrow. (you)

6   My hat is blue. _____ is green. (he)

7   Look at the parrot. _____ feathers are beautiful. (it)

8   The girl always smiles at _____. (I)

9   Kevin is kind. He always helps _____. (we)

WORDS   C kitten 새끼 고양이   country 국가; *시골   necklace 목걸이   D season 계절   parrot 앵무새   feather 깃털

06 This, That, It

This, That, It

1 지시대명사 this, that

❶ 지시대명사 this는 가까이 있는 대상을, that은 멀리 있는 대상을 가리킬 때 쓴다.

this(이것, 이 사람)	that(저 , 저 사람)
This is my book.	**That** is a nice watch.
This is my sister Susan.	**That** is my uncle.

❷ this와 that은 명사 앞에 놓여 지시형용사로도 쓰일 수 있다.

This room is large.　　　　　　　　**That man** is my father.

2 지시대명사 these, those

❶ 둘 이상의 대상을 가리킬 때는 this 대신 these, that 대신 those를 사용한다.

these(이것들, 이 사람들)	those(저것들, 저 사람들)
These are my pens.	**Those** are my puppies.
These are my parents.	**Those** are my friends.

❷ these, those가 지시형용사로 쓰일 경우에는 뒤에 복수명사가 온다.

These apples are fresh.　　　　　　Look at **those clouds**.

3 비인칭 주어 it

시간, 날짜, 요일, 날씨, 명암, 거리 등을 나타낼 때 문장의 주어로 비인칭 주어 it을 쓴다. 이 때 it은 형식적인 주어이므로 '그것'으로 해석하지 않는다.

- **It is 8 o'clock.** 〈시간〉
- **It is March 5.** 〈날짜〉
- **It is Monday.** 〈요일〉

- **It is cold at night.** 〈날씨〉
- **It is dark in here.** 〈명암〉
- **It is 10km from here.** 〈거리〉

✎ NOTE it이 대명사로 쓰일 경우에는 '그것'으로 해석한다.

I have *a toy car*. **It** is my favorite toy.
　　　　　　　　 = a toy car

LET'S CHECK

A   ( ) 안에서 알맞은 말을 고르세요.

0   ((This), These) is my new jacket.

1   (This, These) shoes are comfortable.

2   (This, These) is my brother Jack.

3   (This, These) strawberries are delicious.

4   (This, These) is my favorite song.

5   We need (that, those) boxes.

6   I know (that, those) man.

7   (That, Those) diamond ring is expensive.

8   I really like (that, those) photo.

9   (That, Those) are nice people.

B   밑줄 친 It의 쓰임으로 알맞은 것을 보기에서 고르세요. (중복 가능)

보기	ⓐ 시간	ⓑ 날짜	ⓒ 요일	ⓓ 날씨	ⓔ 거리	ⓕ 명암

0   <u>It</u> is Sunday today.   →   ⓒ

1   <u>It</u> is 5km from here.   →

2   <u>It</u> is very warm today.   →

3   <u>It</u> is the 1st of September.   →

4   <u>It</u> is 10:30.   →

5   <u>It</u> rains a lot in summer.   →

6   <u>It</u> is a 10-minute walk to the station.   →

7   <u>It</u> is too bright in here.   →

WORDS   **A** comfortable 편안한   ring 반지   **B** September 9월   a 10-minute walk 걸어서 10분   station 역

LET'S PRACTICE

A 우리말과 일치하도록 ( ) 안에서 알맞은 말을 고르세요.

0 나는 이 신발이 마음에 든다.
→ I like (this, (these), those) shoes.

1 이 버스는 오늘 매우 붐빈다.
→ (This, These, It) bus is so crowded today.

2 저쪽에 있는 저 남자는 내 삼촌이야.
→ (This, That, Those) man over there is my uncle.

3 이 젤리들은 맛있다.
→ (This, These, Those) jellies are delicious.

4 저 나비들 좀 봐.
→ Look at (that, these, those) butterflies.

5 이것들은 멋진 그림들이다.
→ (This, These, Those) are nice pictures.

B It과 ( ) 안의 말을 이용하여 문장을 완성하세요.

0 _____It is Friday_____ today. (Friday)

1 _____ this morning. (rainy)

2 _____ now. (10:30)

3 _____ today. (a national holiday)

4 _____ from here to the airport. (far)

5 _____ outside. (too dark)

6 _____ tomorrow. (June 25)

WORDS   A crowded 붐비는   B rainy 비가 오는   national holiday 국경일   far 먼, 멀리의   airport 공항

C 그림을 보고 보기에서 알맞은 말을 골라 문장을 완성하세요. (중복 가능)

보기	It	This	That	These	Those

0

_____This_____ is my new bike.

1

Hurry up! _____ is 9 o'clock.

2

_____ building is the post office.

3

_____ are my parents.

4

_____ flowers are for you.

5

_____ is Christmas Day!

D 밑줄 친 부분을 바르게 고치세요.

0 <u>Those</u> car is my neighbor's. → That

1 <u>This</u> is my birthday tomorrow. →

2 Look at <u>that</u> people over there. →

3 <u>This</u> is October 30. →

4 <u>This</u> gloves are warm. →

5 <u>This</u> is Sunday morning. →

6 <u>That</u> girls are my friends. →

7 <u>These</u> bag is heavy. →

WORDS D neighbor 이웃 October 10월

STEP 1

빈칸 완성 빈칸에 알맞은 대명사를 넣어 문장을 완성하세요.

1 그녀와 나는 좋은 친구이다.

→ _____ and _____ are good friends.

2 나는 그들을 매일 본다.

→ I see _____ every day.

3 그는 우리의 새로운 선생님이다.

→ _____ is _____ new teacher.

4 그 빨간 우산은 내 것이다.

→ The red umbrella is _____ .

5 저 사람들은 나의 사촌들이다.

→ _____ are my cousins.

STEP 2

어구 배열 우리말과 일치하도록 ( ) 안의 말을 알맞게 배열하세요.

6 그는 나에게 매일 전화한다. (he, me, calls, every day)

→ _____

7 그녀의 성은 Hong이다. (her, is, Hong, last name)

→ _____

8 그 초록색 집은 그들의 것이다. (the, is, green house, theirs)

→ _____

9 이 코트는 싸다. (this, cheap, coat, is)

→ _____

10 오늘은 토요일이다. (it, Saturday, today, is)

→ _____

STEP 3

영작하기 ( ) 안의 말을 이용하여 우리말을 영어로 옮기세요.

11 너희들은 나의 가장 친한 친구들이다. (are, best friends)

→ _____

12 그는 그의 방에 있다. (is, in, room)

→ _____

13 책상 위에 있는 지갑은 그의 것이다. (the wallet on the desk, is)

→ _____

14 그녀의 부모님은 나를 좋아한다. (parents, like)

→ _____

15 우리는 그들의 도움이 필요하다. (need, help)

→ _____

16 그 샌드위치는 너의 것이다. (the sandwich, is)

→ _____

17 James는 저 건물에서 일한다. (works, in, building)

→ _____

18 이 질문들은 어렵다. (questions, are, difficult)

→ _____

19 오늘은 12월 10일이다. (is, December 10)

→ _____ today.

20 밖에 바람이 많이 분다. (is, windy, outside)

→ _____

REVIEW TEST
CHAPTER 03

1 대명사의 관계가 나머지 넷과 <u>다른</u> 것은?

① I – me   ② we – us
③ he – him   ④ she – hers
⑤ they – them

[2-3] 빈칸에 들어갈 말로 알맞은 것을 고르시오.

2

These are _____ glasses.

① mine   ② you   ③ his
④ she   ⑤ theirs

3

_____ paintings are wonderful.

① It   ② This   ③ That
④ They   ⑤ Those

4 밑줄 친 it의 쓰임이 나머지 넷과 <u>다른</u> 것은?

① <u>It</u> is Tuesday.
② <u>It</u> is November 3.
③ <u>It</u> is sunny today.
④ <u>It</u> is 2km to the beach.
⑤ <u>It</u> is an interesting game.

5 빈칸에 들어갈 말이 순서대로 바르게 짝지어진 것은?

· These presents are _____.
· She always smiles at _____.

① your – I   ② your – me
③ yours – my   ④ you – mine
⑤ yours – me

서술형

[6-7] 빈칸에 알맞은 대명사를 써서 문장을 다시 쓰시오.

6

Sumi and I play badminton on Fridays.

→ _____ play badminton on Fridays.

7

These are her magazines.

→ These magazines are _____.

8 밑줄 친 부분을 가리키는 대명사가 <u>잘못된</u> 것은?

① <u>My sisters</u> are tall. → She
② <u>The movie</u> is boring. → It
③ <u>The man</u> is a singer. → He
④ <u>Children</u> are our future. → They
⑤ <u>You and Tom</u> are my friends. → You

9 밑줄 친 부분의 쓰임이 나머지 넷과 다른 것은?

① It is their job.
② This is Kate's book.
③ He is our new teacher.
④ That baseball cap is his.
⑤ Her name is Kim Jiyoung.

[10-12] 밑줄 친 부분이 잘못된 것을 고르시오.

10 ① The bag is mine.
② I know his address.
③ Ours room is clean.
④ John is very kind to us.
⑤ I meet him every Sunday.

11 ① Look at those men.
② That clouds are big.
③ We live in that house.
④ This is my cousin Jack.
⑤ These are very old coins.

12 ① The clown's nose is red.
② These are Brian's pencils.
③ The birds' nest is in the tree.
④ I don't know the girls's name.
⑤ The handle of the cup is broken.

서술형

[13-14] 어법상 틀린 부분을 찾아 바르게 고치시오.

13
My parents love my sister and I.

_____ → _____

14
That is a nice day today.

_____ → _____

서술형

15 ( ) 안의 단어를 적절한 형태로 바꾸어 문장을 완성하시오.

I have a dog. _____ name is Leo.
(it)

서술형

[16-17] 우리말과 일치하도록 ( ) 안의 말을 이용하여 문장을 완성하시오.

16
이 컴퓨터들은 오래되었고 느리다. (computers)

→ _____ are old
and slow.

17
지금은 7시 30분이다. (7:30)

→ _____ now.

CHAPTER
04

The Verb *Be*
Be동사

LET'S LOOK

I am Sally.

He is Peter.

We are in the same class.

be동사는 주어 뒤에 쓰여 '～이다, ～(에) 있다'의 의미를 나타내는 동사이다.
be동사의 현재형은 주어에 따라 **am, are, is**를 쓴다.

UNIT 07

Be동사의 현재형
Present Simple: *Be*

1 be동사

be동사는 '~이다, ~(에) 있다'의 의미이다. be동사 뒤에는 주로 주어의 상태, 이름이나 직업, 장소를 나타내는 말이 온다.

I **am** *sleepy*.

You **are** *a student*.

My brother **is** *in his room*.

2 be동사의 현재형

❶ be동사의 현재형은 주어에 따라 am, are, is를 쓰고, 「인칭대명사 + be동사」는 줄여 쓸 수 있다.

	주어	be동사	줄임말
단수	I	am	I'm
	You	are	You're
	He/She/It	is	He's/She's/It's
복수	We		We're
	You	are	You're
	They		They're

I am hungry. (= **I'm** hungry.)

She is 15 years old. (= **She's** 15 years old.)

We are at the movie theater. (= **We're** at the movie theater.)

❷ 주어가 명사일 경우에는 단수이면 is, 복수이면 are를 쓴다.

My name **is** Alice.

Peter and Jane **are** at the park.

> **✏ NOTE** 1. **it's vs. its**
> it's는 it is의 줄임말이며, its는 it의 소유격으로 '그것의'란 뜻이다.
>
> I have a dog. **It's** very smart.   I have a dog. **Its** name is Toby.
>   = It is
>
> 2. be동사 뒤에 명사가 올 경우에는 주어에 따라 수가 달라진다.
>
> *He* is **a soccer player**.   *They* are **soccer players**.

LET'S CHECK

A 보기에서 알맞은 be동사를 골라 문장을 완성하세요.

보기	am	are	is

0 She _____ *is* _____ a dentist.

1 I _____ tired.

2 We _____ in the classroom.

3 It _____ my umbrella.

4 They _____ in the kitchen.

5 Your father _____ a police officer.

6 Mike _____ my best friend.

7 The earphones _____ mine.

8 Their garden _____ beautiful.

9 Sam and I _____ good friends.

B 빈칸에 알맞은 be동사의 현재형과 줄임말을 각각 쓰세요.

0 He   *is*   →   *He's*

1 I   →

2 You   →

3 It   →

4 They   →

5 She   →

6 We   →

3 be동사의 부정문

「be동사 + not」의 형태이며, '~가 아니다, ~(에) 있지 않다'의 의미이다.

	주어	be동사 + not	줄임말	
단수	I	am not	I'm not	
	You	are not	You're not	You aren't
	He/She/It	is not	He's/She's/It's not	He/She/It isn't
복수	We		We're not	We aren't
	You	are not	You're not	You aren't
	They		They're not	They aren't

I am not sick.

She's not my English teacher.

They aren't at the library now.

> **NOTE** am not은 amn't로 줄여 쓰지 않는다.
> **I amn't** sick. [×] → **I'm not** sick. [○]

4 be동사의 의문문

「be동사 + 주어 ~?」의 형태이며, '~이니?, ~(에) 있니?'의 의미이다.

	의문문	긍정의 대답	부정의 대답
단수	Am I ~?	Yes, you are.	No, you aren't.
	Are you ~?	Yes, I am.	No, I'm not.
	Is he/she/it ~?	Yes, he/she/it is.	No, he/she/it isn't.
복수	Are we ~?	Yes, we/you are.	No, we/you aren't.
	Are you ~?	Yes, we are.	No, we aren't.
	Are they ~?	Yes, they are.	No, they aren't.

A: **Are you** a photographer?

B: **Yes, I am. / No, I'm not.**

A: **Is Mr. Kim** in the classroom?

B: **Yes, he is. / No, he isn't.**

> **NOTE** be동사 의문문의 주어가 this/that, these/those일 경우, 대답은 it이나 they를 주어로 쓴다.
> A: Is **this** your book?   B: Yes, **this** is. [×] → Yes, **it** is. [○]
> A: Are **these** your books?   B: Yes, **these** are. [×] → Yes, **they** are. [○]

LET'S CHECK

C 빈칸에 be동사 현재형의 부정형과 그 줄임말을 각각 쓰세요.

0   He ____is not____ my uncle.   →   He ____isn't____ my uncle.

1   We _____ ready.   →   We _____ ready.

2   She _____ busy today.   →   She _____ busy today.

3   I _____ a hairdresser.   →   _____ a hairdresser.

4   They _____ in class.   →   They _____ in class.

5   This _____ my smartphone.   →   This _____ my smartphone.

6   Jack and Jake _____ twins.   →   Jack and Jake _____ twins.

7   The keys _____ in my bag.   →   The keys _____ in my bag.

D ( ) 안의 말과 be동사를 이용하여 현재형 의문문과 대답을 완성하세요.

0   A: _____Is she_____ a new student? (she)
    B: Yes, _____she is_____ .

1   A: _____ a good singer? (you)
    B: No, _____ .

2   A: _____ cold outside? (it)
    B: Yes, _____ .

3   A: _____ late for school? (I)
    B: No, _____ .

4   A: _____ hot? (this soup)
    B: Yes, _____ .

5   A: _____ expensive? (the tickets)
    B: No, _____ .

WORDS   C hairdresser 미용사   twin 쌍둥이   D ticket 표, 입장권

LET'S PRACTICE

A ( ) 안에서 알맞은 말을 고르세요.

0   It (is, am) warm today.

1   We (am, are) very lucky.

2   Mr. Jones (am, is) in the hospital.

3   This (is, are) a nice computer.

4   They (is, are) from Australia.

5   Cathy and I (am, are) at the mall.

6   Ann and Sue (is, are) sisters.

7   My father (am, is) at home today.

8   The dogs (are, is) in the doghouse.

9   My family and I (are, am) on vacation.

B be동사 현재형의 부정형과 줄임말을 써서 문장을 완성하세요.

0   The boy _____isn't_____ honest.

1   I'm healthy. _____ sick.

2   The children _____ at the zoo.

3   My coat _____ in the closet.

4   These boxes _____ empty.

5   The dishes _____ clean.

6   Our living room _____ very big.

7   Whales _____ fish.

8   My brother _____ at school.

9   They _____ my boots.

WORDS   A lucky 운이 좋은   on vacation 휴가 중인   B healthy 건강한   closet 옷장   empty 빈, 비어 있는   dish 접시   whale 고래

C 그림을 보고 be동사를 이용하여 현재형 의문문과 대답을 완성하세요.

0

A: _____Is_____ he a singer?

B: ___No___, _____he isn't_____. He is a magician.

1

A: _____ you cold?

B: _____, _____.

2

A: _____ it sunny?

B: _____, _____.

3

A: _____ you and your father on a plane?

B: _____, _____.

D 밑줄 친 주어를 복수형으로 바꾸어 문장을 다시 쓰세요.

0	It is my pencil.	→	They are my pencils.
1	I am a middle school student.	→	
2	Her little sister is cute.	→	
3	You are a good doctor.	→	
4	Is he a famous actor?	→	
5	The tree is not green.	→	

WORDS C magician 마술사   plane 비행기   cute 귀여운

08 There is/are

UNIT

There is/are

1 There is/are의 의미와 형태

❶ There is/are는 '~가 있다'의 의미이다. 이때 There는 '거기에'라고 해석하지 않는다.

❷ There is/are는 be동사 뒤에 주어가 나오며, 주어의 수에 따라 is 또는 are를 쓴다.

There is + 단수명사	There are + 복수명사	There is + 셀 수 없는 명사
There is *a clock*.	**There are** *five crayons*.	**There is** *some sugar*.

2 There is/are의 부정문

「There is/are + not + 주어」의 형태이며, '~가 있지 않다'의 의미이다. is not과 are not은 각각 isn't, aren't로 줄여 쓸 수 있다.

There is not *a cloud* in the sky.

There aren't *many books* on the shelf.

3 There is/are의 의문문

「Is/Are there + 주어 ~?」의 형태이며, '~가 있니?'의 의미이다.

A: **Is there** *a TV* in the living room?

B: **Yes, there is. / No, there isn't.**

A: **Are there** *children* in the pool?

B: **Yes, there are. / No, there aren't.**

(+PLUS) 1. any(약간의, 조금도)는 There is/are의 부정문과 의문문에서 자주 쓰인다. any 뒤에는 셀 수 있는 명사의 복수형이나 셀 수 없는 명사가 온다.

A: Are there **any** *apples* on the tree? B: No, there aren't **any** *apples*.

A: Is there **any** *milk* in the bottle? B: No, there isn't **any** *milk*.

2. 긍정문에서는 any 대신 some을 사용한다.

There are **some** *apples* on the tree.

There is **some** *milk* in the bottle.

LET'S CHECK

A 빈칸에 is/are 또는 isn't/aren't를 넣어 문장을 완성하세요.

| 긍정문 | | 부정문 | |

0 There _____is_____ a dog.

1 There _____ boxes.

2 There _____ a ball.

3 There _____ five men.

4 There _____ some salt.

5 There _____ some eggs.

6 There _____ one apple.

7 There _____ flowers.

8 There _____ some bread.

9 There _____ many fish.

0 There _____isn't_____ any water.

10 There _____ any children.

11 There _____ any money.

12 There _____ any books.

13 There _____ a bus stop.

14 There _____ any milk.

15 There _____ any students.

16 There _____ a cup.

17 There _____ any food.

18 There _____ any pictures.

B 주어진 문장을 이용하여 의문문과 대답을 완성하세요.

0 There is a chair in this room.

  → A: _____Is there_____ a chair in this room?   B: Yes, _____there is_____ .

1 There are books in your bag.

  → A: _____ books in your bag?   B: No, _____ .

2 There is meat in the shop.

  → A: _____ meat in the shop?   B: Yes, _____ .

3 There are people in the pool.

  → A: _____ people in the pool?   B: Yes, _____ .

4 There is juice in the bottle.

  → A: _____ juice in the bottle?   B: No, _____ .

WORDS   **B** pool 수영장 (= swimming pool)

LET'S PRACTICE

 A 그림을 보고 There is/isn't 또는 There are/aren't를 넣어 문장을 완성하세요.

0
_____There is_____ a kite in the sky.

1
_____ two birds on the branch.

2
_____ any money in my wallet.

3
_____ three people in the car.

4
_____ an elevator in this building.

5
_____ two cars on the road.

6
_____ a hole in my sock.

7
_____ any children on the playground.

WORDS A branch 나뭇가지 wallet 지갑 elevator 엘리베이터 playground 놀이터

B 그림을 보고 There is 또는 There are를 이용하여 대화를 완성하세요. (필요하면 형태를 바꿔서 쓸 것)

0

A: _____Is there_____ a car in the garage?

B: ___Yes___, _____there is_____.

1

A: _____ any letters in the mailbox?

B: _____, _____.

2

A: _____ candles on the cake?

B: _____, _____.

3

A: _____ any food in the refrigerator?

B: _____, _____.

C ( ) 안에서 알맞은 말을 고르세요.

0   There is ((a ball), two balls) in the box.

1   There is (a window, two windows) in this room.

2   There are (an egg, some eggs) in the basket.

3   There is (a good movie, good movies) on TV tonight.

4   Is there (a zoo, zoos) in your city?

5   Are there (a question, any questions)?

6   There aren't (a picture, any pictures) on the wall.

7   There isn't (a computer, many computers) in the classroom.

8   There are (a cup of tea, two cups of tea) on the table.

WORDS   B garage 차고   mailbox 우편함   candle 양초   question 질문

STEP 1

빈칸 완성 빈칸에 알맞은 be동사를 넣어 문장을 완성하세요.

1 Bill과 Mike는 축구팀이다.

→ Bill and Mike _____ on the soccer team.

2 이 채소들은 신선하지 않다.

→ These vegetables _____ fresh.

3 A: 나는 너의 가장 친한 친구니? B: 응, 맞아.

→ A: _____ I your best friend? B: Yes, you _____ .

4 거실에 피아노가 한 대 있다.

→ There _____ a piano in the living room.

5 그 상점에는 손님들이 많이 있다.

→ There _____ many customers in the shop.

STEP 2

어구 배열 우리말과 일치하도록 ( ) 안의 말을 알맞게 배열하세요.

6 이것은 내 책이다. (book, is, my, this)

→ _____

7 그들은 지금 서울에 있지 않다. (they, not, in Seoul, are)

→ _____ now.

8 그들은 너희 부모님이니? (they, are, parents, your)

→ _____

9 차 안에 아기가 있다. (baby, there, a, in the car, is)

→ _____

10 1년은 365일이 있다. (are, 365 days, there, in a year)

→ _____

STEP 3

영작하기 ( ) 안의 말을 이용하여 우리말을 영어로 옮기세요.

11 그는 훌륭한 피아니스트이다. (a great pianist)

→ _____

12 너와 나는 다르다. (different)

→ _____

13 그의 이름은 흔하지 않다. (name, common)

→ _____

14 그들은 체육관에 없다. (at the gym)

→ _____

15 A: 이것은 네 셔츠니? B: 응, 맞아. (your shirt)

→ A: _____ B: _____

16 A: David와 Chris는 형제니? B: 아니, 그렇지 않아. (brothers)

→ A: _____ B: _____

17 문에 누군가 있다. (there, someone, at the door)

→ _____

18 방에 탁자 한 개와 의자 두 개가 있다. (there, a table and two chairs, in the room)

→ _____

19 주전자에 물이 하나도 없다. (there, any, water, in the kettle)

→ _____

20 A: 교실에 선생님이 계시니? B: 응, 계셔. (there, a teacher, in the classroom)

→ A: _____ B: _____

1 밑줄 친 부분의 의미가 나머지 넷과 다른 것은?

① This is my hat.
② He is an engineer.
③ They are in my bag.
④ We are good friends.
⑤ I am fourteen years old.

서술형

[2-3] 빈칸에 알맞은 be동사를 넣어 문장을 완성하시오.

2
_____ your father a writer?

3
There _____ four people in my family.

4 밑줄 친 부분이 잘못된 것은?

① She is busy today.
② We are in the garden.
③ Mr. Wilson is a doctor.
④ Jason and I am classmates.
⑤ The children are at school now.

5 밑줄 친 부분이 옳은 것은?

① He are from Japan.
② Their house are big.
③ Mary am my best friend.
④ You and your sister is tall.
⑤ The actress is very beautiful.

[6-7] 빈칸에 들어갈 말로 알맞지 않은 것을 고르시오.

6
_____ are good students.

① We   ② You
③ They   ④ The boys
⑤ John

7
There is _____ on the table.

① a book   ② juice
③ onions   ④ an apple
⑤ some butter

8 밑줄 친 부분의 줄임말이 잘못된 것은?

① I amn't a singer.
② We aren't at home.
③ They're not American.
④ She's not here right now.
⑤ It isn't my phone number.

9 다음 우리말을 영어로 바르게 옮긴 것은?

그들은 의사가 아니다.

① They isn't a doctor.
② They aren't a doctor.
③ They not are doctors.
④ They are not doctors.
⑤ They're aren't doctors.

10 다음 중 대화가 자연스럽지 <u>않은</u> 것은?

① A: Am I right?

B: Yes, you are.

② A: Is this Tom's backpack?

B: Yes, he is.

③ A: Is Mrs. Yoon your teacher?

B: No, she isn't.

④ A: Are you and Sally at home?

B: Yes, we are.

⑤ A: Are the boys at the water park?

B: No, they aren't.

11 대화의 빈칸에 들어갈 말로 알맞은 것은?

A: Are you an only child?

B: _____. I have a brother.

① No, I am. ② Yes, I am.

③ No, I'm not. ④ Yes, I'm not.

⑤ No, you aren't.

12 다음 중 어법상 옳지 <u>않은</u> 문장은?

① There is a bird in the tree.

② There is some tea in the cup.

③ There isn't any toys in the box.

④ Is there a bookstore near here?

⑤ Are there cars in the parking lot?

13 어법상 틀린 부분을 찾아 바르게 고치시오.

A: Are there lions at the zoo?

B: Yes, they are.

_____ → _____

[14-17] 우리말과 일치하도록 ( ) 안의 말을 이용하여 문장을 완성하시오.

14

그 멜론은 달지 않다 (sweet)

→ The melon _____.

15

Chris과 Alex는 차에 있니? (Chris and Alex)

→ _____ in the car?

16

치즈 옆에 생쥐 한 마리가 있다. (a mouse)

→ _____ next to the cheese.

17

공원에 사람들이 많이 있습니까? (many people)

→ _____ in the park?

CHAPTER
05

Present Simple
현재시제

LET'S LOOK

I **walk** to school every day.

Spring **comes** after winter.

현재시제는 현재의 일반적인 사실, 반복적인 습관, 변함없는 진리를 나타낸다.
일반동사의 현재형은 동사원형 또는 동사원형에 **-(e)s**를 붙여 만든다.

09 일반동사의 현재형 1
Present Simple 1

1 일반동사

일반동사는 be동사와 조동사를 제외한 나머지 동사로 주어의 동작이나 상태를 나타낸다.

- 동작 동사　　go, jump, eat, play, read …
- 상태 동사　　love, like, want, have, know …

2 일반동사의 현재형

❶ 일반동사의 현재형은 현재의 일반적인 사실, 반복적인 습관, 변함없는 진리를 나타낸다.

Ann **lives** in New York. 　　 I **get** up at 7 a.m. 　　 Water **boils** at 100°C.

❷ 일반동사의 현재형은 주어가 3인칭 단수일 때 동사원형에 -(e)s를 붙인다.

I/You/We/They	동사원형
He/She/It	동사원형 + -(e)s

I *read* books every day. → He **reads** books every day.

They *watch* TV in the evening. → She **watches** TV in the evening.

3 일반동사의 3인칭 단수 현재형 만들기

대부분의 동사	+ -s	run → run**s**	work → work**s**
-o, -s, -x, -ch, -sh로 끝나는 동사	+ -es	do → do**es**　　　go → go**es** pass → pass**es**　　fix → fix**es** teach → teach**es**　brush → brush**es**	
〈자음 + y〉로 끝나는 동사	y를 i로 고치고 + -es	cry → cr**ies**　　study → stud**ies** 〈모음 + y〉는 + -s: enjoy**s**, play**s**, stay**s**	
예외	have → **has**		

Sue **studies** Chinese on Fridays.

My brother **has** a turtle as a pet.

LET'S CHECK

A 주어진 동사의 3인칭 단수 현재형을 쓰세요.

0	write	writes	10	have	_____
1	eat	_____	11	listen	_____
2	drive	_____	12	snow	_____
3	cry	_____	13	try	_____
4	enjoy	_____	14	miss	_____
5	like	_____	15	walk	_____
6	speak	_____	16	help	_____
7	make	_____	17	fly	_____
8	finish	_____	18	do	_____
9	teach	_____	19	stay	_____

B 주어진 동사의 현재형을 써서 문장을 완성하세요.

0 ride
   (1) The boys _____ride_____ their bikes.
   (2) The boy _____rides_____ his bike.

1 go
   (1) We _____ hiking on Sundays.
   (2) He _____ hiking on Sundays.

2 wash
   (1) I _____ my hair every day.
   (2) She _____ her hair every day.

3 study
   (1) They _____ English very hard.
   (2) Jake _____ English very hard.

4 play
   (1) Bob and Kevin _____ basketball after school.
   (2) Bob _____ basketball after school.

WORDS   A write 쓰다   try 노력하다   stay 머무르다, 있다

LET'S PRACTICE

A   ( ) 안에서 알맞은 말을 고르세요.

0   Oliver usually (wear, (wears)) jeans.

1   Mary (do, does) yoga every morning.

2   My neighbor (have, has) a big dog.

3   The children (eat, eats) lunch at noon.

4   We (sit, sits) on chairs.

5   Mr. Smith (start, starts) work at 8 a.m.

6   Julie and I often (go, goes) to the city library.

7   He (drink, drinks) a glass of water every morning.

8   My sister (like, likes) comic books.

9   You (speak, speaks) Korean very well.

B   ( ) 안에 주어진 동사의 현재형을 써서 문장을 완성하세요.

0   My dad ____drives____ me to school. (drive)

1   You _____ an apple with a knife. (cut)

2   Sally _____ chocolate ice cream. (like)

3   Time _____ fast. (fly)

4   Kimberly usually _____ at home on Sundays. (stay)

5   Many people _____ in the city. (live)

6   My dog _____ in my bed. (sleep)

7   He always _____ the exams. (pass)

8   Mr. Kim _____ history at a high school. (teach)

9   Amy _____ her cat's fur every day. (brush)

WORDS   A usually 보통, 대개   do yoga 요가를 하다   sit 앉다   comic book 만화책   B cut 자르다   exam 시험   history 역사   fur 털

C 그림을 보고 ( ) 안에 주어진 동사의 현재형을 써서 문장을 완성하세요.

0   1    2    3

0   Sue _____*has*_____ a special talent. She _____*paints*_____ very well. (have, paint)

1   Greg _____ at a bakery. He _____ bread. (work, make)

2   Alex _____ an exam tomorrow. He _____ nervous. (have, feel)

3   My aunt _____ in Paris. I _____ her every summer. (live, visit)

D 밑줄 친 부분이 맞으면 O를 쓰고, 틀리면 바르게 고치세요.

0   My school <u>has</u> a cafeteria.   →   *O*

1   Kate <u>is change</u> her hair color often.   →

2   My family and I <u>go</u> to a hot spring in winter.   →

3   Tom always <u>trys</u> his best.   →

4   My mother <u>drinks</u> tea in the morning.   →

5   Many people <u>enjoys</u> K-pop these days.   →

6   John <u>washs</u> his car on Sundays.   →

7   Carol <u>eat</u> dinner at home.   →

8   Koalas <u>live</u> in Australia.   →

9   My parents <u>goes</u> to bed at 10 p.m.   →

WORDS   C talent 재능   bakery 빵집, 제과점   nervous 불안한, 초조한   D cafeteria 카페테리아, 구내식당   change 바꾸다   hot spring 온천
try[do] one's best 최선을 다하다

10

일반동사의 현재형 2
Present Simple 2

1 일반동사 현재형의 부정문

「do not/does not + 동사원형」의 형태이며, '~하지 않는다'의 의미이다.

I/You/We/They	do not (= don't)	동사원형
He/She/It	does not (= doesn't)	

I **like** sweets and chocolate. → I **don't like** sweets and chocolate.

My mother **works** at a hospital. → My mother **doesn't work** at a hospital.

> **NOTE** do not/does not 뒤에는 반드시 동사원형이 와야 한다.
> My mother **doesn't works** at a hospital. [×]

2 일반동사 현재형의 의문문

「Do/Does + 주어 + 동사원형?」의 형태이며, '~하니?'의 의미이다.

의문문			긍정의 대답	부정의 대답
Do	I		Yes, you do.	No, you don't.
	you		Yes, I/we do.	No, I/we don't.
	we		Yes, we/you do.	No, we/you don't.
	they	동사원형?	Yes, they do.	No, they don't.
Does	he		Yes, he does.	No, he doesn't.
	she		Yes, she does.	No, she doesn't.
	it		Yes, it does.	No, it doesn't.

A: **Do you take** a shower every day?

B: **Yes, I do. / No, I don't.**

A: **Does she go** to school by bus?

B: **Yes, she does. / No, she doesn't.**

> **NOTE** 일반동사의 부정문과 의문문을 만들 때 사용하는 do와 does는 조동사이다. 일반동사 do(하다)와 혼동하지 않도록 주의하자.
> Tom *does* his homework every day. → Tom **doesn't** *do* his homework every day.
> **Does** Tom *do* his homework every day?

LET'S CHECK

A   ( ) 안에서 알맞은 말을 고르세요.

0   John (don't, (doesn't)) like his job.

1   I (don't, doesn't) believe in magic.

2   Amanda (don't, doesn't) wear a necklace.

3   My father (don't, doesn't) talk a lot.

4   My grandparents (don't, doesn't) work anymore.

5   Mr. Yoon (don't, doesn't) live in Seoul.

6   We (don't, doesn't) read newspapers.

7   Some children (don't, doesn't) enjoy sports.

8   Jim (don't, doesn't) do his homework.

9   They (don't, doesn't) speak English. They speak French.

B   ( ) 안에서 알맞은 말을 고르고 빈칸에 알맞은 말을 넣어 대화를 완성하세요.

0   A: ((Do), Does) you write letters?   B: No, ____I don't____ .

1   A: (Do, Does) your father cook?   B: Yes, _____ .

2   A: (Do, Does) we need more food?   B: No, _____ .

3   A: (Do, Does) it rain a lot in summer?   B: Yes, _____ .

4   A: (Do, Does) they learn Chinese at school? B: Yes, _____ .

5   A: (Do, Does) Mr. Kim work on Saturdays?   B: No, _____ .

6   A: (Do, Does) the cat like fish?   B: Yes, _____ .

7   A: (Do, Does) the shops sell shoes?   B: No, _____ .

8   A: (Do, Does) you and Bill know each other? B: Yes, _____ .

WORDS   **A** believe in (~의 존재를) 믿다   magic 마법, 마술   anymore 더 이상   newspaper 신문   **B** sell 팔다   each other 서로

LET'S PRACTICE

A   보기에서 알맞은 말을 골라 don't/doesn't와 함께 써서 현재형 부정문을 완성하세요. (단, 한 번씩만 쓸 것)

보기	drive	have	know	~~like~~	need	teach

0   Bill _____doesn't like_____ skiing. He likes snowboarding.

1   Our car is only two years old. We _____ a new car.

2   He _____ to work. He goes to work by bus.

3   I _____ her name. Do you know it?

4   Mrs. Han _____ English. She teaches math.

5   Tracy is an only child. She _____ any brothers or sisters.

B   주어진 문장을 부정문과 의문문으로 바꿔 쓰세요. (줄임말을 쓸 것)

0   James fixes computers.
   (1) 부정문: _____James doesn't fix computers._____
   (2) 의문문: _____Does James fix computers?_____

1   Lucy buys many clothes.
   (1) 부정문: _____
   (2) 의문문: _____

2   The bus comes every hour.
   (1) 부정문: _____
   (2) 의문문: _____

3   Rachel and Jay play tennis together.
   (1) 부정문: _____
   (2) 의문문: _____

WORDS   A only child 외동   B fix 고치다   every hour 매시간

C 그림을 보고 ( ) 안의 말을 이용하여 현재형 의문문과 대답을 완성하세요.

0

A: _____Does_____ she _____go_____ to bed before 11:00? (go)

B: _____Yes_____, _____she does_____.

1

A: _____ Tim and Sarah _____ school uniforms? (wear)

B: _____, _____.

2

A: _____ you _____ fruit for dessert? (have)

B: _____, _____.

3

A: _____ your laptop _____ well? (work)

B: _____, _____.

D 밑줄 친 부분을 바르게 고치세요.

0 I <u>no</u> like fish. → don't

1 We <u>have not</u> classes today. →

2 My parents <u>doesn't</u> watch TV. →

3 Dave <u>isn't</u> come home late. →

4 Alice doesn't <u>drinks</u> coffee. →

5 <u>Has he</u> a good idea? →

6 <u>They go</u> to the same school? →

7 Does he <u>knows</u> your e-mail address? →

8 <u>Does</u> your friends have smartphones? →

WORDS   C dessert 디저트, 후식   laptop 휴대용 컴퓨터, 노트북   work 일하다; *작동하다   address 주소

11 Be동사 vs. 일반동사
Verbs in the Present Simple

1 ## be동사와 일반동사의 현재형

❶ be동사의 현재형은 '~이다, ~(에) 있다'의 의미로, 주어에 따라 am, are, is를 쓴다.

❷ 일반동사는 주어의 동작이나 상태를 나타내는 동사로 뜻이 다양하다. 주어에 따라 동사원형을 쓰거나 동사원형에 -(e)s를 붙인다.

	be동사		일반동사	
I	am	I		run
You/We/They	are	You/We/They		
He/She/It	is	He/She/It		runs

Amy **is** a good dancer. She **dances** well.

Ken and Liz **are** at the library. They **study** together.

> **✎ NOTE** 주어가 명사일 때 be동사와 일반동사의 현재형
>
> | | be동사 | 일반동사 |
> |---|---|---|
> | 복수 | The students **are** smart. | The students **like** math. |
> | 단수 | The student **is** smart. | The student **likes** math. |

2 ## be동사와 일반동사 현재형의 부정문과 의문문

❶ be동사의 부정문은 「be동사 + not」, 의문문은 「be동사 + 주어 ~?」의 형태이다.

❷ 일반동사는 조동사 do/does를 이용하여 부정문과 의문문을 만든다.

	be동사	일반동사
부정문	am/are/is + not	do not/does not + 동사원형
의문문	Am/Are/Is + 주어 ~?	Do/Does + 주어 + 동사원형?

A: She **is not** Korean. **Is she** American?

B: **Yes, she is. / No, she isn't.**

A: He **doesn't walk** to school. **Does he go** to school by bus?

B: **Yes, he does. / No, he doesn't.**

LET'S CHECK

A

( ) 안에 주어진 동사의 현재형을 써서 문장을 완성하세요.

0   I _____like_____ pizza. (like)

1   I _____ in class now. (be)

2   He _____ up early in the morning. (get)

3   We _____ students. (be)

4   My grandparents _____ in the country. (live)

5   The toy shop _____ at 9:00 p.m. (close)

6   My brothers _____ always nice to me. (be)

7   Margaret _____ children's books. (write)

8   My dog's name _____ Einstein. (be)

9   Ellen and her sister _____ well. (sing)

B

( ) 안에서 알맞은 말을 고르세요.

0   I (am not, don't) a good cook.

1   Paul (doesn't, isn't) drive a car.

2   Cathy (doesn't, isn't) in her room now.

3   (Do, Are) you busy today?

4   (Do, Are) they listen to pop music?

5   They (aren't, don't) live in this town.

6   I (don't, am not) go for a walk at night.

7   (Do, Are) you and Sally have the same birthday?

8   A: (Do, Are) you a doctor? B: No, I (don't, am not).

9   A: (Do, Are) you like seafood? B: Yes, I (do, am).

WORDS   B go for a walk 산책하러 가다   at night 밤에   seafood 해산물

LET'S PRACTICE

A

빈칸에 들어갈 말로 알맞은 것을 고르세요.

0 I _____ sick today. I have a cold.

　✓ⓐ am　　　　ⓑ are　　　　ⓒ do　　　　ⓓ does

1 James _____ his homework after school.

　ⓐ is　　　　ⓑ are　　　　ⓒ do　　　　ⓓ does

2 My sister's hair _____ very long.

　ⓐ am not　　ⓑ isn't　　　ⓒ don't　　　ⓓ doesn't

3 The machines _____ work well.

　ⓐ isn't　　　ⓑ aren't　　　ⓒ don't　　　ⓓ doesn't

4 _____ Don and Julia at school?

　ⓐ Is　　　　ⓑ Are　　　　ⓒ Do　　　　ⓓ Does

5 _____ Ann visit her grandparents every month?

　ⓐ Is　　　　ⓑ Are　　　　ⓒ Do　　　　ⓓ Does

6 _____ Mr. and Mrs. Green live near your house?

　ⓐ Is　　　　ⓑ Are　　　　ⓒ Do　　　　ⓓ Does

B

자연스러운 대화가 되도록 알맞게 연결하세요.

0 Are you hungry? •　　　　　　　• ⓐ Yes, we do.

1 Is she your sister? •　　　　　　• ⓑ No, I don't.

2 Is the cat on the mat? •　　　　　• ⓒ Yes, it is.

3 Do you listen to the radio? •　　　• ⓓ No, I'm not.

4 Does your mom work? •　　　　　• ⓔ No, she isn't.

5 Do we have time for lunch? •　　　• ⓕ Yes, she does.

WORDS　A cold 추운; *감기　machine 기계　near 근처에, 가까이에

C 보기에서 알맞은 동사를 골라 적절한 형태로 바꾸어 문장을 완성하세요. (현재형으로 쓸 것)

0  1  2  3

보기	be (x4)	cut	work	play	feed

0 I ____am____ a farmer. I ____work____ on a farm.

1 You _____ a zookeeper. You _____ animals.

2 He _____ a hairdresser. He _____ people's hair.

3 They _____ musicians. They _____ musical instruments.

D ( ) 안에서 알맞은 말을 고르세요.

0 (Are, (Do)) penguins fly?

1 He doesn't (drive, drives) a car.

2 My grandmother (isn't, doesn't) wear glasses.

3 (Are, Do) they speak English?

4 (Is, Does) it rain a lot in summer?

5 Kevin sometimes (doesn't, doesn't do) his homework.

6 They (aren't, don't) my friends.

7 These answers (aren't, don't) correct.

8 That (isn't, doesn't) my apartment building.

9 The sun (isn't, doesn't) rise in the west.

WORDS C feed 먹이를 주다 farmer 농부 farm 농장 zookeeper 사육사 musical instrument 악기 D penguin 펭귄
correct 맞는, 정확한 rise (해가) 뜨다 west 서쪽

빈칸 완성 ( ) 안의 말을 이용하여 문장을 완성하세요.

1 그는 우리집 근처에 산다. (live)

→ He _____ near my house.

2 그 말들은 매우 빨리 달린다. (run)

→ The horses _____ very fast.

3 그는 오페라를 즐기지 않는다. (enjoy)

→ He _____ operas.

4 코알라들은 나뭇잎들을 좋아하니? (like)

→ _____ koalas _____ leaves?

5 Mary는 은행에서 일하니? (work)

→ _____ Mary _____ at a bank?

어구 배열 우리말과 일치하도록 ( ) 안의 말을 알맞게 배열하세요.

6 그는 인터넷으로 책을 구입한다. (he, books, buys, on the Internet)

→ _____

7 그들은 토요일마다 탁구를 친다. (they, table tennis, on Saturdays, play)

→ _____

8 그녀는 내 이름을 기억하지 못한다. (doesn't, name, she, my, remember)

→ _____

9 너는 매일 머리를 감니? (do, wash, your, you, hair, every day)

→ _____

10 김 선생님은 프랑스어를 가르치시니? (Mr. Kim, French, teach, does)

→ _____

STEP 3

영작하기 ( ) 안의 말을 이용하여 우리말을 영어로 옮기세요.

11 Rachel과 나는 함께 점심을 먹는다. (Rachel and I, eat, lunch, together)

→ _____

12 학교는 3시 30분에 끝난다. (school, finish, at 3:30)

→ _____

13 우리는 저녁에 산책을 하러 간다. (go for a walk, in the evening)

→ _____

14 그는 방학 동안 해외여행을 간다. (travel abroad, during his vacation)

→ _____

15 내 여동생은 공포영화를 보지 않는다. (my sister, watch, horror movies)

→ _____

16 아이들은 커피를 마시지 않는다. (children, drink, coffee)

→ _____

17 그 에어컨은 잘 작동하지 않는다. (the air conditioner, work, well)

→ _____

18 그들은 서로 아는 사이니? (know, each other)

→ _____

19 너희 아버지는 설거지를 하시니? (your father, wash, the dishes)

→ _____

20 그 식당은 아침 식사를 제공하니? (the restaurant, serve, breakfast)

→ _____

REVIEW TEST
CHAPTER 05

1 동사의 3인칭 단수 현재형이 <u>잘못</u> 연결된 것은?

① fix – fixes   ② live – lives

③ buy – buys   ④ miss – misses

⑤ finish – finishs

2 빈칸에 들어갈 말이 순서대로 바르게 짝지어진 것은?

> · My parents _____ breakfast at 7.
>
> · The baby _____ every night.

① have – cry   ② has – cry

③ have – crys   ④ has – cries

⑤ have – cries

서술형

[3-4] ( ) 안의 동사를 알맞은 형태로 쓰시오.
(단, 현재형으로 쓸 것)

3

> Ted _____ his teeth after meals.
> (brush)

4

> The scientist _____ the universe.
> (study)

5 빈칸에 들어갈 말로 알맞지 <u>않은</u> 것은?

> _____ lives in this town.

① Mike

② The girl

③ Their uncle

④ His grandmother

⑤ Mr. and Mrs. Kim

6 다음 중 어법상 옳지 <u>않은</u> 문장은?

① The train travels fast.

② They want a new house.

③ The girl has a pretty doll.

④ The Earth goes around the sun.

⑤ Mary and Paul plays table tennis.

7 다음 문장을 부정문으로 바르게 고친 것은?

> He walks his dog every day.

① He walk not his dog every day.

② He isn't walk his dog every day.

③ He don't walks his dog every day.

④ He doesn't walk his dog every day.

⑤ He doesn't walks his dog every day.

8 빈칸에 들어갈 말로 알맞은 것은?

> John lives near his school. He walks
> to school. He _____ take a bus
> to school.

① not   ② isn't   ③ does

④ don't   ⑤ doesn't

9 빈칸에 들어갈 말이 나머지 넷과 <u>다른</u> 것은?

① _____ your brother tall?

② _____ Yumi get up early?

③ _____ she like ice cream?

④ _____ Henry play the violin?

⑤ _____ he wear a school uniform?

10 다음 중 대화가 자연스럽지 <u>않은</u> 것은?

① A: Do you exercise every day?
   B: No, I don't.
② A: Do you and Jane like hamburgers?
   B: Yes, we do.
③ A: Does your father teach history?
   B: Yes, he does.
④ A: Do they go skiing in winter?
   B: No, they aren't.
⑤ A: Does Mrs. Lynn speak Korean?
   B: Yes, she does.

11 빈칸에 들어갈 말로 알맞은 것은?

A: Does she have a pet?
B: _____

① Yes, she is.
② Yes, she do.
③ No, she isn't.
④ No, she does.
⑤ No, she doesn't.

서술형

[12-13] 빈칸에 알맞은 말을 써서 대화를 완성하시오.

12

A: _____ _____ know Nick?
B: Yes, I do. He is my classmate.

13

A: Does the amusement park have a roller coaster?
B: Yes, _____ _____.

서술형

[14-15] 다음 문장을 (   ) 안의 지시대로 바꿔 쓰시오.

14

She likes traveling by plane. (부정문)

→ She _____ traveling by plane.

15

They play soccer after school. (의문문)

→ _____ soccer after school?

서술형

[16-17] 우리말과 일치하도록 (   ) 안의 말을 이용하여 문장을 완성하시오.

16

나는 일요일에는 숙제를 하지 않는다. (do)

→ I _____ my homework on Sundays.

17

너는 매일 일기를 쓰니? (keep)

→ _____ a diary every day?

CHAPTER
06

Prepositions
전치사

LET'S LOOK

He is **in** the swimming pool.

I have breakfast **at** 8 o'clock.

전치사는 명사나 대명사 앞에 쓰여 장소, 시간 등을 나타내는 말이다. 전치사는 **at, on, in, under, for, from, to** 등이 있으며 한 전치사가 여러 가지 의미로 사용되기도 한다.

UNIT 12 장소를 나타내는 전치사
Prepositions of Place

1 전치사

전치사는 명사나 대명사 앞에 쓰여 장소, 시간 등을 나타내는 말이다.

There is a mirror **on** the wall.

The show starts **at** 7:30.

> **NOTE** 전치사 뒤에 대명사가 올 경우에는 목적격을 사용한다.
>
> **with** *he* [×]   **with** *his* [×]   **with** *him* [○]

2 at, on, in

at, on, in은 대표적인 장소의 전치사이다. at은 특정 지점, on은 접촉한 표면의 위, in은 공간의 내부 또는 도시, 국가 등 비교적 넓은 장소를 나타낸다.

at(~에)	on(~ 위에)	in(~ 안에, ~에)
at the desk	**on** the table	**in** the car
at the door	**on** the shelf	**in** my bedroom
at the bus stop	**on** the wall	**in** Seoul
at home/school/work	**on** the floor	**in** Italy

3 기타 장소를 나타내는 전치사

under(~ 아래에)   above(~ 위에)   in front of(~ 앞에)   behind(~ 뒤에)

next to(~ 옆에)   between(~ 사이에)   across from(~ 맞은편에)

> **NOTE** between은 「between + 복수명사」 또는 「between A and B」 형식으로 쓰인다.
>
> The river flows **between** *two mountains*.
>
> The library is **between** *the bank and the post office*.

LET'S CHECK

A 빈칸에 at, on, in 중 알맞은 전치사를 넣어 문장을 완성하세요.

0

My friend lives
_____*in*_____ Seoul.

1

The painting is
_____ the wall.

2

The clothes are
_____ the basket.

3

They are _____
the bus stop.

4

The teacher is
_____ her desk.

5

The candles are
_____ the cake.

B 보기에서 알맞은 말을 골라 우리말을 영어로 옮기세요.

보기	above	under	behind	in front of
	next to	between	across from	

0 구름 위에   →   _____*above*_____ the clouds

1 커튼 뒤에   →   _____ the curtain

2 나무 아래   →   _____ the tree

3 내 옆에   →   _____ me

4 그 건물 앞에   →   _____ the building

5 학교와 공원 사이에 →   _____ the school and the park

6 주유소 맞은편에   →   _____ the gas station

7 두 집 사이에   →   _____ the two houses

WORDS   B curtain 커튼   gas station 주유소

LET'S PRACTICE

A   그림을 보고 빈칸에 알맞은 전치사를 넣어 문장을 완성하세요.

0

The bird is _____in_____ the cage.

1

The pots are _____ the gas stove.

2

The deliveryman is _____ the door.

3

The airplane is _____ the sea.

4

The truck is _____ the taxi.

5

The river flows _____ the bridge.

6

The pencil is _____ the eraser and the ruler.

7

Ann sits _____ me in class.

WORDS   A cage 새장   pot 냄비   gas stove 가스레인지   deliveryman 배달원   flow 흐르다   bridge 다리

B 그림과 일치하도록 알맞게 연결하세요.

0   The clock is   •   • ⓐ under the table.

1   The fireplace is   •   • ⓑ next to the sofa.

2   The sofa is   •   • ⓒ between the lamps.

3   The table is   •   • ⓓ above the fireplace.

4   The cat is   •   • ⓔ in front of the sofa.

5   The window is   •   • ⓕ behind the TV.

6   The toy box is   •   • ⓖ across from the TV.

C 밑줄 친 부분을 바르게 고치세요.

0   There is a steak <u>in</u> the plate.   →   on

1   The Sahara Desert is <u>at</u> Africa.   →

2   My father is <u>on</u> work now.   →

3   There is a clock <u>next</u> the window.   →

4   There is someone <u>behind of</u> me.   →

5   The bus stop is <u>in front from</u> the school. →

6   The restaurant is <u>across of</u> the bookstore. →

7   His office is between the bank <u>or</u> the hospital. →

WORDS   B clock 시계   fireplace 벽난로   lamp 램프, 등   C plate 접시

UNIT 13

시간을 나타내는 전치사
Prepositions of Time

1 at, on, in

at, on, in은 시간을 나타내는 전치사로도 쓰인다. at은 구체적인 시각이나 하루의 특정 시점 앞에 쓴다. on은 날짜, 요일, 특정한 날 앞에 쓴다. in은 월, 연도, 계절, 오전/오후/저녁 등 비교적 긴 시간 앞에 쓴다.

at 9 o'clock

on January 1

in December

at	on	in
at 7 o'clock	**on** April 25	**in** July
at noon	**on** Monday(s)	**in** 2020
at night	**on** Christmas Day	**in** summer
at midnight	**on** Sunday morning	**in** the morning/afternoon/evening

> **NOTE**
> 1. 대체로 at, on, in이 나타내는 시간 범위는 at < on < in의 순서로 넓어진다.
>   **at** 7 o'clock (시각) < **on** Monday (요일) < **in** July (월)
>
> 2. this, next, last, every, today, tomorrow 앞에는 시간을 나타내는 전치사 at, on, in을 쓰지 않는다.
>   We have a party **on this Friday**. [×] → We have a party **this Friday**. [○]
>   I meet her **in every morning**. [×] → I meet her **every morning**. [○]

2 기타 시간을 나타내는 전치사

before	~ 전에	We study together **before** tests.
after	~ 후에	He watches TV **after** dinner.
for + 기간의 길이	~ 동안	The baby sleeps **for** *fifteen hours* a day.
during + 특정 기간	~ 동안, ~ 중에	I turn off my cellphone **during** *a movie*.
until	~까지 (계속)	The museum is open **until** 9 p.m.
from A to B	A부터 B까지	I study English **from** 7:00 **to** 8:00.

LET'S CHECK

ANSWER KEY p.10

A

빈칸에 at, on, in 중 알맞은 것을 쓰세요.

0	__on__ March 11		10	_____ noon
1	_____ 1999		11	_____ night
2	_____ the morning		12	_____ Saturday
3	_____ 8 o'clock		13	_____ September 25
4	_____ spring		14	_____ summer
5	_____ June		15	_____ 09:30
6	_____ June 30		16	_____ the afternoon
7	_____ Tuesday		17	_____ Monday afternoon
8	_____ New Year's Day		18	_____ midnight
9	_____ January		19	_____ my birthday

B

보기에서 알맞은 말을 골라 우리말을 영어로 옮기세요.

보기	before	after	for	during	until	from	to

0	방과 후에	→	__after__ school
1	취침 전에	→	_____ bedtime
2	회의 중에	→	_____ the meeting
3	9시부터 10시까지	→	_____ 9:00 _____ 10:00
4	5일 동안	→	_____ five days
5	10월 31일까지	→	_____ October 31
6	방학 동안	→	_____ vacation
7	여러 해 동안	→	_____ many years

WORDS   A New Year's Day 1월 1일, 새해 첫날   midnight 자정   B bedtime 취침 시

LET'S PRACTICE

A   빈칸에 at, on, in 중 알맞은 전치사를 넣어 문장을 완성하세요.

0   The summer festival is _____in_____ July.

1   My birthday is _____ October 3.

2   Many flowers bloom _____ spring.

3   It gets cold _____ night.

4   The fireworks start _____ 8 p.m.

5   Our school closes _____ Teacher's Day.

6   We usually have lunch _____ noon.

7   Jane goes to church _____ Sundays.

8   John and I play tennis _____ Saturday afternoon.

9   The alarm clock rings _____ 7:30 _____ the morning.

B   ( ) 안에서 알맞은 말을 고르세요.

0   He comes home ((before), for) 8 o'clock.

1   The city buses run (in, until) midnight.

2   Susan drinks tea (after, from) lunch.

3   Fall comes (before, after) summer.

4   Julie practices the violin (for, during) 2 hours every day.

5   Our lunchtime is from 12 (before, to) 1 o'clock.

6   Some animals sleep (from, during) the winter.

7   It is dark (before, after) sunrise.

8   John takes a shower (during, after) exercise.

9   David works (at, from) 9:00 a.m. to 5:00 p.m.

WORDS   A festival 축제   bloom 꽃이 피다   fireworks 불꽃놀이   alarm clock 자명종   ring 울리다   B run 달리다; *운행하다
sunrise 해돋이, 일출

C Amy의 방과 후 일과표를 보고 보기에서 알맞은 말을 골라 문장을 완성하세요. (단, 한 번씩만 쓸 것)

4:00 p.m. – 5:00 p.m.	take a piano lesson
6:00 p.m. – 7:00 p.m.	do homework
7:00 p.m. – 8:00 p.m.	have dinner
8:00 p.m. – 9:00 p.m.	watch TV
9:00 p.m. – 10:00 p.m.	read some books

보기
before
after
for
until
~~from~~
~~to~~

0 Amy takes a piano lesson ____from____ 4:00 p.m. ____to____ 5:00 p.m.

1 She does her homework _____ dinner.

2 _____ dinner, she watches TV _____ an hour.

3 She reads some books _____ 10:00 p.m.

D 밑줄 친 부분을 바르게 고치세요.

0 The first class starts <u>on</u> 9:00 a.m. → at

1 I get sleepy <u>on</u> the afternoon. →

2 Many people don't work <u>at</u> Sunday. →

3 Peter usually goes skiing <u>on</u> January. →

4 The kids get presents <u>at</u> Children's Day. →

5 In Australia, Christmas is <u>at</u> summer. →

6 Mary watches TV <u>in</u> Sunday evening. →

7 Jack usually takes a nap <u>during</u> 30 minutes. →

8 We have classes <u>at</u> 9 to 4 o'clock. →

9 My mother's birthday is <u>on tomorrow</u>. →

WORDS D sleepy 졸리는 present 선물 take a nap 낮잠을 자다

STEP 1

빈칸 완성 보기에서 알맞은 말을 골라 문장을 완성하세요.

보기	at	on	in	under	until

1 Tom은 학교에 친구들이 많이 있다.

→ Tom has a lot of friends _____ school.

2 그 중식당은 2층에 있다.

→ The Chinese restaurant is _____ the second floor.

3 그 선물들은 크리스마스 트리 아래에 있다.

→ The presents are _____ the Christmas tree.

4 농부들은 봄에 씨를 심는다.

→ Farmers plant seeds _____ spring.

5 그 축제는 7월 30일까지 계속된다.

→ The festival lasts _____ July 30.

STEP 2

어구 배열 우리말과 일치하도록 ( ) 안의 말을 알맞게 배열하세요.

6 나는 그녀 앞에 앉는다. (her, sit, front, in, I, of)

→ _____

7 도서관은 병원 맞은편에 있다. (library, from, the, is, hospital, across, the)

→ _____

8 그는 해가 뜨기 전에 집을 나선다. (home, he, sunrise, leaves, before)

→ _____

9 Emily는 아침 6시에 일어난다. (gets up, in, 6 o'clock, at, morning, Emily, the)

→ _____

10 그녀는 월요일부터 금요일까지 일한다. (Monday, works, from, Friday, she, to)

→ _____

STEP 3

영작하기 ( ) 안의 말을 이용하여 우리말을 영어로 옮기세요.

11 네 양말은 서랍 속에 있다. (your socks, the drawer)

→ _____

12 주차장은 건물 뒤에 있다. (the parking lot, the building)

→ _____

13 그 버스는 서울역 앞에 정차한다. (the bus, stop, Seoul Station)

→ _____

14 그 강은 두 나라 사이를 흐른다. (the river, flow, two countries)

→ _____

15 그 경기는 정오에 시작한다. (the game, start, noon)

→ _____

16 우리는 5월에 학교 소풍을 간다. (go on a school picnic, May)

→ _____

17 나는 자정 전에 잠자리에 든다. (go to bed, midnight)

→ _____

18 Mike는 퇴근 후에 체육관에 간다. (go to the gym, work)

→ _____

19 Sara는 매일 30분 동안 요가를 한다. (do yoga, 30 minutes, every day)

→ _____

20 그는 방학 동안 뉴욕에 머무른다. (stay, New York, his vacation)

→ _____

[1-3] 빈칸에 들어갈 말로 알맞은 것을 고르시오.

1

> Robert lives _____ Seoul.

① at   ② on   ③ in
④ to   ⑤ from

2

> Jane's birthday is _____ May 10.

① at   ② on   ③ in
④ for   ⑤ under

3

> My cat goes out _____ night.

① at   ② on   ③ in
④ for   ⑤ until

4 두 문장의 뜻이 같도록 할 때 빈칸에 알맞은 것은?

> The hotel is in front of the bank.
> → The bank is _____ the hotel.

① in   ② under   ③ behind
④ between   ⑤ next to

5 빈칸에 들어갈 말이 순서대로 바르게 짝지어진 것은?

> · Bats sleep _____ the day.
> · She washes the dishes _____ 30 minutes.

① on – until   ② for – for
③ during – for   ④ for – during
⑤ during – during

[6-7] 밑줄 친 부분이 잘못된 것을 고르시오.

6
① Beijing is on China.
② My bag is in the car.
③ They sing on the stage.
④ The children play in the park.
⑤ There is someone at the door.

7
① School starts in March.
② The train leaves at 7:00 a.m.
③ The weather is hot in summer.
④ The museum opens on this Friday.
⑤ We have a party on New Year's Day.

8 빈칸에 들어갈 말로 알맞지 않은 것은?

> There is a chair next to _____.

① she   ② me   ③ him
④ Mike   ⑤ the sofa

[9-10] 빈칸에 공통으로 들어갈 말을 고르시오.

9

· The balls are _____ the box.
· I wear gloves _____ winter.

① at   ② on   ③ in
④ from   ⑤ between

10

· There are some tents _____
  the grass.
· They play tennis _____ Sunday
  afternoon.

① at   ② on   ③ in
④ before   ⑤ behind

서술형

[11-12] ( ) 안의 말을 알맞게 배열하여 문장을 완성하
시오.

11

제과점은 카페 맞은편에 있다.
(from, the bakery, across, is, the café)

→ _____

12

우리는 크리스마스 이브에 양말을 걸어둔다.
(hang up, on, socks, we, Christmas Eve)

→ _____

서술형

[13-15] Tom의 시간표를 보고 빈칸에 알맞은 전치사를
쓰시오.

11:00 a.m. – 12:00 p.m.	Math
12:00 p.m. – 1:00 p.m.	Lunch
1:00 p.m. – 2:00 p.m.	English
2:00 p.m. – 3:00 p.m.	Music

13

Tom has math class _____ lunch.

14

Tom has a music class _____
English class.

15

Tom has lunch _____ 12:00 p.m.
_____ 1:00 p.m.

서술형

[16-17] 우리말과 일치하도록 ( ) 안의 말을 이용하여
문장을 완성하시오.

16

지붕 아래 새 둥지 하나가 있다. (the roof)

→ There is a bird's nest

_____.

17

그 셔츠는 7월 10일까지 할인 판매한다. (July 10)

→ The shirt is on sale

_____.

CHAPTER
07

Adjectives, Adverbs
형용사와 부사

LET'S LOOK

A giraffe has a **long** neck.

She dances **beautifully**.

형용사는 '둥근, 빨간, 예쁜, 작은'처럼 사람이나 사물의 성질, 모습 등을 나타내는 말이다. 형용사는 **명사**를 더 자세하고 다양하게 설명해주는 역할을 한다.

부사는 '빠르게, 일찍, 아름답게, 매우' 등과 같은 말로, 문장에서 **동사**, **형용사**, **다른 부사**, 또는 **문장 전체**를 꾸며주는 역할을 한다.

14 형용사
Adjectives

1 형용사

❶ 형용사는 사람이나 사물의 성질, 모습 등을 나타내는 말이다. 형용사를 사용하면 명사를 더 구체적으로 설명할 수 있다.

- a table   →   a **round** table
- a building   →   a **tall** building
- a child   →   a **happy** child

❷ 형용사는 명사 앞에 쓰여 명사를 꾸며주거나, 동사 뒤에 쓰여 주어를 보충 설명해준다.

형용사 + 명사	동사 + 형용사
I live in a **big** *city*.	Mr. Kim *is* **kind**.
He likes **spicy** *food*.	The sky *looks* **clear** today.

> **✎ NOTE**
>
> 1. -thing, -body, -one으로 끝나는 말은 형용사가 뒤에서 꾸며준다.
>
>   I want *something* **cold**.   There is *someone* **new** in this room.
>
> 2. 형용사와 함께 쓰이는 동사
>
>   be(~이다), become/get/turn(~이 되다, ~해지다), look(~하게 보이다), feel(~하게 느끼다),
>   sound(~하게 들리다), smell(~한 냄새가 나다), taste(~한 맛이 나다) 등
>
>   Leaves *turn* **green** in spring.   This soup *smells* **delicious**.

2 자주 쓰이는 형용사

hot – cold	good – bad	short – long	busy
fast – slow	happy – sad	easy – hard, difficult	angry
small – big, large	rich – poor	old – new, young	honest
strong – weak	clean – dirty	cheap – expensive	delicious
noisy – quiet	hungry – full	kind – rude	favorite
dry – wet	sick – healthy	bright – dark	famous

> **+PLUS** 명사 앞에 형용사가 2개 이상 올 경우에는 수량 > 의견(beautiful, delicious, kind 등) > 크기 > 색 > 재료 순서로 쓴다.
>
> her **beautiful blue** eyes   **five small red** tomatoes   **a white wooden** chair

LET'S CHECK

A 주어진 문장에서 형용사를 모두 찾아 동그라미 하세요.

0 I like (cold) weather.

1 My aunt has a cute, brown puppy.

2 Balloons are light.

3 He is a lucky guy.

4 The apples aren't cheap.

5 I want the purple crayon.

6 Skydiving is a dangerous sport.

7 They have two young children.

8 The old man looks kind.

9 Your new dress is lovely.

B 보기에서 알맞은 말을 골라 문장을 완성하세요. (단, 한 번씩만 쓸 것)

보기	fresh	~~old~~	warm

0 Rome has a(n) _____old_____ history.

1 Stella buys _____ vegetables at the market.

2 It is cold outside. You need a(n) _____ coat.

보기	simple	tired	salty

3 Seawater tastes _____.

4 This game is very _____.

5 I often feel _____ after school.

WORDS　A light 가벼운　cheap 값이 싼　purple 자주색의　dangerous 위험한　young 어린　B salty 소금이 든, 짠　seawater 바닷물

LET'S PRACTICE

A 주어진 형용사와 반대의 뜻을 가진 말을 보기에서 골라 빈칸에 쓰세요.

보기	clean poor	~~sad~~ cold	healthy cheap	noisy ugly	light short	safe wrong

0	happy	_____sad_____	**6**	heavy	_____
1	dirty	_____	**7**	rich	_____
2	quiet	_____	**8**	beautiful	_____
3	long	_____	**9**	hot	_____
4	expensive	_____	**10**	sick	_____
5	right	_____	**11**	dangerous	_____

B 그림을 보고 보기에서 알맞은 말을 골라 문장을 완성하세요. (단, 한 번씩만 쓸 것)

0  **1** **2**  **3**

보기	difficult	good	hot	lazy	~~strong~~	thirsty

0 The man has big arms. He is a _____strong_____ man.

1 Look at that panda bear. It looks _____ .

2 It is a _____ day. I am _____ .

3 She isn't _____ at math. It is _____ for her.

WORDS A noisy 시끄러운 safe 안전한 poor 가난한 ugly 못생긴 wrong 틀린 dirty 더러운 quiet 조용한 right 옳은
B lazy 게으른 be good at ~을 잘하다

C ( ) 안의 형용사가 들어갈 곳에 ✓로 표시하세요.

0 (expensive)　　This watch is too✓.

1 (long)　　The pianist has fingers.

2 (angry)　　Mr. Kim looks today.

3 (interesting)　　This is an idea.

4 (big)　　Bob drives a bus.

5 (busy)　　The workers are.

6 (great)　　My mom's apple pie tastes.

7 (enough)　　We don't have money.

8 (dangerous)　　Snakes are animals.

9 (young)　　The businessman is rich.

D 두 문장의 뜻이 같도록 빈칸에 알맞은 말을 써서 문장을 완성하세요.

0 The knife is sharp.　　=　　It is _____ a sharp knife _____.

1 The skirt is blue.　　=　　It is _____.

2 The boy is smart.　　=　　He is _____.

3 The rule is important.　　=　　It is _____.

4 The actor is famous.　　=　　He is _____.

5 The roses are pink.　　=　　They are _____.

6 The trucks are huge.　　=　　They are _____.

7 The woman is wise.　　=　　She is _____.

8 The present is special.　　=　　It is _____.

9 The names are common.　　=　　They are _____.

WORDS　C finger 손가락　enough 충분한　businessman 사업가　D sharp 날카로운　rule 규칙　huge 거대한, 매우 큰　wise 현명한 common 흔한

UNIT 15 부사
Adverbs

1 부사

❶ 부사는 시간, 장소, 방법, 정도 등을 나타내는 말이다.

시간	today, yesterday, now, later …	방법	fast, slowly, hard, well, kindly …
장소	here, there, home, outside …	정도	so, very, quite, really, too …

❷ 부사는 동사, 형용사, 다른 부사, 문장 전체를 꾸며준다.

동사 + 부사	She *smiles* **happily**.
부사 + 형용사	That is a **really** *good* idea.
부사 + 부사	The boy runs **very** *fast*.
부사 + 문장 전체	**Luckily**, *I have nice teachers*.

2 부사의 형태

대부분의 부사	형용사 +-ly	bad → bad**ly** quick → quick**ly** nice → nice**ly** careful → careful**ly**
-le로 끝나는 형용사	e를 빼고 +-y	simple → simp**ly** terrible → terrib**ly**
-y로 끝나는 형용사	y를 i로 고치고 +-ly	easy → eas**ily** happy → happ**ily** busy → bus**ily** lucky → luck**ily**
형용사와 형태가 같은 부사	fast (빠른 – 빨리) late (늦은 – 늦게)	high (높은 – 높이) early (이른 – 일찍) hard (어려운; 열심히 하는 – 열심히)
예외	good → **well**	

John drives **carefully**.

I can answer the question **easily**.

They work very **hard**.

/NOTE 1. 형용사에 -ly가 붙었지만 뜻이 달라지거나, 형용사와 형태가 같지만 뜻이 다른 부사도 있으므로 주의한다.

lately 최근에　　hardly 거의 ~않는　　highly 매우　　pretty 꽤, 매우

2. -ly로 끝나지만 부사가 아니라 형용사인 경우

friendly 상냥한　　lovely 사랑스러운　　lonely 외로운　　weekly 매주의　　monthly 매월의

LET'S CHECK

 A 주어진 문장에서 부사를 모두 찾아 동그라미 하세요.

0 Those birds fly (high).

1 The children play outside.

2 Susan greets her teachers politely.

3 This question is pretty difficult.

4 His jokes are really funny.

5 Finally, the exam is over.

6 The girls dance very well.

7 Some of my friends live here.

8 My father comes home early on Wednesday.

9 David solves math problems easily.

B 주어진 형용사를 부사로 바꿔 쓰세요.

0	happy	happily	10	easy	_____
1	slow	_____	11	beautiful	_____
2	safe	_____	12	quiet	_____
3	loud	_____	13	busy	_____
4	soft	_____	14	simple	_____
5	fast	_____	15	clear	_____
6	terrible	_____	16	early	_____
7	angry	_____	17	kind	_____
8	quick	_____	18	noisy	_____
9	hard	_____	19	good	_____

WORDS A greet 인사하다 politely 예의 바르게 joke 농담 finally 마침내 over 끝난 solve 풀다, 해결하다   B soft 부드러운
terrible 끔찍한 angry 화가 난 quick 빠른

LET'S PRACTICE

A ( ) 안에서 알맞은 말을 고르세요.

0   The baby smiles (sweet, (sweetly)).

1   My mom is always (busy, busily).

2   The children play (happy, happily) together.

3   Jane always talks (quiet, quietly).

4   The doll looks (real, really).

5   The frog jumps (high, highly).

6   Those candles smell really (good, well).

7   (Lucky, Luckily), I have a free ticket to the concert.

8   George cooks (terrible, terribly).

9   This room has a (nice, nicely) view.

B 그림을 보고 보기에서 알맞은 말을 골라 문장을 완성하세요. (단, 한 번씩만 쓸 것)

0	1	2	3

보기	fast	hard	~~slowly~~	softly

0   The snail moves very _____slowly_____ .

1   Ants are diligent. They work very _____ .

2   I like express trains. They run _____ .

3   My cat is so tiny. I touch the cat _____ .

WORDS   A doll 인형   real 진짜의   view 전망   B snail 달팽이   diligent 근면한, 부지런한   express train 급행열차   tiny 아주 작은

C ( ) 안의 말을 적절한 형태로 바꾸어 빈칸에 쓰세요.

0 He always dresses _____neatly_____. (neat)

1 The man walks too _____. (fast)

2 Jane sleeps _____ at night. (deep)

3 The birds sing _____. (beautiful)

4 George _____ loves his wife. (true)

5 Roy swims very _____. (good)

6 The bus sometimes arrives _____. (late)

7 They play the music so _____. (loud)

8 Susan is smart. She learns everything _____. (quick)

9 My parents eat healthy food. They eat _____. (healthy)

D 밑줄 친 부분을 바르게 고치세요.

0 Kevin paints so <u>bad</u>.　　　　　　→　　　　　　　badly

1 The museum closes <u>lately</u>.　　　　→

2 Anna plays the piano very <u>good</u>.　　→

3 The firefighters are <u>bravely</u>.　　　→

4 He comes to school <u>earlily</u>.　　　　→

5 The stars shine <u>bright</u>.　　　　　　→

6 They live together <u>happy</u>.　　　　　→

7 His father is an <u>honestly</u> man.　　　→

8 It is <u>warm pretty</u> today.　　　　　　→

9 Do you study English <u>hardly</u>?　　　→

WORDS C dress 옷을 입다 neat 단정한 deep 깊은 true 진실의 arrive 도착하다 D bad 나쁜, 형편없는 bravely 용감하게
shine 빛나다

16 수량 형용사, 빈도부사
Quantifiers, Frequency Adverbs

1 수량 형용사

명사 앞에 쓰여 명사의 수나 양이 많고 적음을 나타내는 말이다. many, much, a lot of, (a) few, (a) little, some, any 등이 있다.

2 many/much/a lot of, (a) few/(a) little

	셀 수 있는 명사 앞	셀 수 없는 명사 앞
많은	**many** books	**much** water
	a lot of books	**a lot of** water
몇 개의, 조금의	**a few** books	**a little** water
거의 없는	**few** books	**little** water

I have **many** friends. 나는 친구가 많다.

She doesn't drink **much** coffee. 그녀는 커피를 많이 마시지 않는다.

A few students know the answer. 학생들 몇 명이 그 답을 안다.

We have **little** time. 우리는 시간이 거의 없다.

> **NOTE** 1. 긍정문에서는 much 대신 a lot of를 쓰는 것이 더 자연스럽다.
>
> He has **a lot of** money.　　　　He doesn't have **much** money.
>
> 2. many, a lot of, (a) few 뒤에 오는 셀 수 있는 명사는 복수형을 쓴다.
>
> **many** *students*　　　　**a lot of** *people*　　　　**a few** *pencils*

3 some, any

some	긍정문	I have **some** apples/milk. (몇 개의, 조금의)
	부정문	I don't have **any** apples/milk. (전혀, 조금도)
any	의문문	Do you have **any** apples/milk? (몇 개의, 조금의)

> **NOTE** 1. 권유를 나타내는 의문문에서는 some을 쓴다.
>
> Do you want **some** apples/milk?
>
> 2. some, any 뒤에 오는 셀 수 있는 명사는 복수형을 쓴다.
>
> **some** *eggs*　　　　**any** *books*　　　　**some** *women*

LET'S CHECK

A

( ) 안에서 알맞은 말을 고르세요.

0   (many, (much)) time

1   (a few, a little) potatoes

2   (many, a lot of) milk

3   (few, little) rice

4   (many, little) textbooks

5   (much, a lot of) people

6   (a little, many) money

7   (many, much) homework

8   (a few, a little) umbrellas

9   (a few, a little) chocolate

B

빈칸에 some 또는 any를 넣어 문장을 완성하세요.

0   I see _____ some _____ cows in the field.

1   Do you have _____ good ideas?

2   We watch _____ TV in the evening.

3   I don't have _____ brothers or sisters.

4   The baseball player doesn't make _____ mistakes.

5   Do you want _____ orange juice?

6   Is there _____ food in the refrigerator?

7   I really need _____ advice.

8   She doesn't drink _____ coffee.

9   Are there _____ eggs in the basket?

WORDS   A textbook 교과서   B cow 소   field 들판   mistake 실수   advice 조언, 충고

4 빈도부사

❶ 빈도부사는 어떤 일이 얼마나 자주 일어나는지를 나타내는 부사이다.

(0%) never	rarely	sometimes	often	usually	always (100%)
결코 ~않다	거의 ~않다	가끔, 때때로	자주, 종종	보통, 대개	항상

❷ rarely, never는 이미 부정의 의미를 포함하고 있으므로 not과 함께 쓰지 않는다.

My grandfather **doesn't rarely** get angry. [×]

My grandfather **rarely** gets angry. [○]

Mike **doesn't never** break his promise. [×]

Mike **never** breaks his promise. [○]

5 빈도부사의 위치

❶ 빈도부사는 be동사 뒤, 일반동사 앞에 쓰인다.

She *is* **never** in a hurry.

He **usually** *wears* jeans and sneakers.

❷ 의문문에서는 빈도부사가 주어 뒤에 온다.

Do *you* **often** help your mother?

Is *he* **sometimes** late for school?

LET'S CHECK

C ( ) 안의 정보를 참고하여 보기에서 알맞은 말을 골라 문장을 완성하세요. (단, 한 번씩만 쓸 것)

보기	always	~~usually~~	often	sometimes	rarely	never

0 (80%)   My father _____usually_____ cooks dinner.

1 (100%)   John _____ wears a suit to work.

2 (40%)   They _____ eat dinner at restaurants.

3 (60%)   Rick and Susie _____ play tennis together.

4 (0%)   Jane is _____ late for school.

5 (20%)   I _____ write letters to my friends.

D ( ) 안의 말을 알맞은 곳에 넣어 문장을 다시 쓰세요.

0   I take a shower in the morning. (always)

→ _____I always take a shower in the morning._____

1   We go to the beach in summer. (often)

→ _____

2   They are busy on Mondays. (usually)

→ _____

3   Rachel cooks Italian food. (sometimes)

→ _____

4   David takes a taxi. (rarely)

→ _____

5   The shop is open on weekends. (never)

→ _____

WORDS   **C** suit 정장

LET'S PRACTICE

A 주어진 수량 형용사 뒤에 올 수 있는 명사를 고르세요.

0	many	☑ children	☐ duck
1	few	☐ house	☐ buses
2	a little	☐ tea	☐ computer
3	some	☐ book	☐ trees
4	a lot of	☐ apple	☐ eggs
5	much	☐ snow	☐ boxes
6	a lot of	☐ monkey	☐ cheese
7	a few	☐ balls	☐ homework
8	any	☐ meat	☐ potato
9	little	☐ shoes	☐ sugar

B 보기에서 알맞은 말을 하나씩 골라 대화를 완성하세요.

보기	some	~~any~~
	some	any

보기	money	~~help~~
	cake	people

0 A: Do you need _____ any help _____?

   B: No, I'm fine. I can do it myself.

1 A: Do you want _____?

   B: Oh, thank you. It looks delicious.

2 A: The stadium is empty. I don't see _____.

   B: Right. There is no game today.

3 A: Oh, no. I didn't bring my wallet.

   B: Don't worry. I have _____.

WORDS B stadium 경기장 bring 가져오다 worry 걱정하다

C 우리말과 일치하도록 few/a few 또는 little/a little을 넣어 문장을 완성하세요.

0 나는 돈이 거의 없다. → I have ____little____ money.

1 물이 약간 있다. → There is _____ water.

2 책이 몇 권 있다. → There are _____ books.

3 John은 친구가 거의 없다. → John has _____ friends.

4 그들에게 희망이 조금 있다. → They have _____ hope.

5 우리는 시간이 거의 없다. → We have _____ time.

6 학생들이 조금 있다. → There are _____ students.

7 공기가 거의 없다. → There is _____ air.

D 다음 Tom의 일과표를 보고 보기에서 알맞은 말을 골라 문장을 완성하세요. (단, 한 번씩만 쓸 것)

	Mon	Tue	Wed	Thu	Fri	Sat	Sun
get up at 7:00	O	O	O	O	O		
eat breakfast	O	O	O	O	O	O	O
go to the gym	O		O		O		O
be late for school							
play computer games		O		O		O	

보기   always   ~~usually~~   often   sometimes   never

0 Tom _____usually gets up at 7:00_____.

1 He _____.

2 He _____.

3 He _____.

4 He _____.

WORDS   C hope 희망

STEP 1

보기 완성 보기에서 알맞은 말을 골라 문장을 완성하세요.

보기	early	loud	quiet	safely	heavily

1 나는 조용한 방을 원한다.

→ I want a(n) _____ room.

2 그 꽃들은 이른 봄에 핀다.

→ The flowers bloom in _____ spring.

3 내 차에서 시끄러운 소리가 난다.

→ My car makes a(n) _____ noise.

4 7월에는 때때로 비가 많이 내린다.

→ It sometimes rains _____ in July.

5 밤에는 안전 운전 하세요.

→ Please drive _____ at night.

STEP 2

어구 배열 우리말과 일치하도록 ( ) 안의 말을 알맞게 배열하세요.

6 대기오염은 심각한 문제이다. (air pollution, a, problem, serious, is)

→ _____

7 Dave는 중국어를 매우 잘 한다. (speaks, Dave, Chinese, well, very)

→ _____

8 많은 관광객들이 그 도시를 방문한다. (a, tourists, the, lot, visit, of, city)

→ _____

9 그 소녀는 오렌지 몇 개가 필요하다. (a, oranges, the, needs, girl, few)

→ _____

10 의사들은 보통 흰색 가운을 입는다. (wear, white, doctors, usually, gowns)

→ _____

영작하기 ( ) 안의 말을 이용하여 우리말을 영어로 옮기세요.

11 네팔에는 높은 산들이 있다. (Nepal, have, high, mountains)

→ _____

12 그 보드게임은 쉬워 보인다. (the board game, look, easy)

→ _____

13 그 발레리나들은 우아하게 춤춘다. (the ballerinas, dance, graceful)

→ _____

14 솔직히, 나는 그의 이름이 기억나지 않는다. (honest, not, remember, name)

→ _____

15 그는 자유시간이 많지 않다. (not, have, free time)

→ _____

16 그녀는 외국어를 전혀 못한다. (not, speak, foreign language)

→ _____

17 디저트 좀 드시겠어요? (want, dessert)

→ _____

18 사막에는 물이 거의 없다. (there, water, in the desert)

→ _____

19 그 가수를 아는 사람들은 거의 없다. (people, know, the singer)

→ _____

20 지하철은 아침에 항상 북적거린다. (the subway, crowded, in the morning)

→ _____

1 두 단어의 관계가 나머지 넷과 다른 것은?

① true – truly   ② bad – badly
③ easy – easily   ④ quick – quickly
⑤ week – weekly

[2-4] 빈칸에 들어갈 말로 알맞지 않은 것을 고르시오.

2
Jane is a very _____ girl.

① kind   ② smart   ③ nicely
④ lovely   ⑤ good

3
The man looks _____.

① old   ② young   ③ angry
④ friendly   ⑤ happily

4
Mike drives _____.

① fastly   ② safely   ③ slowly
④ carefully   ⑤ well

[5-7] 다음 중 어법상 옳지 않은 문장을 고르시오.

5 ① The towels are wet.
② I like sunny weather.
③ He tells funny stories.
④ My dad likes his old car.
⑤ I want special something.

6 ① He feels very sick.
② She looks beautiful.
③ This soup smells good.
④ The music sounds sadly.
⑤ The medicine tastes bitter.

7 ① He goes to bed early.
② The cat moves silently.
③ The bus often comes lately.
④ She practices the piano hard.
⑤ The teacher speaks very clearly.

8 밑줄 친 pretty의 뜻이 나머지 넷과 다른 것은?

① She has a pretty face.
② They are pretty dresses.
③ The food is pretty good.
④ You look so pretty today.
⑤ Their new house is pretty.

9 빈칸에 들어갈 말이 순서대로 바르게 짝지어진 것은?

· The city has _____ museums.

· Ali doesn't spend _____ money.

① many – little   ② a few – little

③ many – much   ④ a little – a lot of

⑤ a lot of – many

10 빈칸에 공통으로 들어갈 수 있는 말은?

· Peter has _____ old coins.

· Do you want _____ apple juice?

① a few   ② any   ③ some

④ many   ⑤ much

11 밑줄 친 부분이 옳은 것은?

① They have few bread.

② She writes many letter.

③ I remember any names.

④ We have a little minutes.

⑤ We don't eat much food.

12 다음 우리말을 영어로 바르게 옮긴 것은?

그는 학교에 절대 늦지 않는다.

① He is late for school never.

② He is never late for school.

③ He never is late for school.

④ He isn't never late for school.

⑤ He never isn't late for school.

서술형

13 ( ) 안의 말을 알맞게 배열하여 문장을 완성하시오.

(she, friends, a, has, of, lot, good)

→ _____

서술형

14 어법상 틀린 부분을 고쳐 문장을 다시 쓰시오.

I eat usually toast for breakfast.

→ _____

서술형

[15-17] 우리말과 일치하도록 ( ) 안의 말을 이용하여
문장을 완성하시오.

15

그 농구 선수는 매우 높이 뛴다. (high)

→ The basketball player jumps very

_____.

16

그녀는 물을 거의 마시지 않는다. (little, water)

→ She drinks _____.

17

Alex는 하루에 몇 시간씩 운동을 한다. (few, hour)

→ Alex exercises _____

a day.

MEMO

MEMO

MEMO

MEMO

MEMO

MEMO

Your Best Friend on the Way to Becoming a Grammar Master

Grammar Mate 1

WORKBOOK

DARAKWON

Grammar Mate 1

WORKBOOK

Contents

UNIT 01 셀 수 있는 명사 Countable Nouns

A 주어진 명사를 단수형은 복수형으로, 복수형은 단수형으로 쓰세요.

0	pencil	–	pencils	10	–	buses
1	watch	–		11	–	photos
2	map	–		12	–	babies
3	roof	–		13	–	wolves
4	foot	–		14	–	oxen
5	tomato	–		15	–	mice
6	dish	–		16	–	horses
7	class	–		17	–	heroes
8	lady	–		18	–	parties
9	day	–		19	–	knives

B 주어진 명사를 ( ) 안의 말과 함께 써서 문장을 완성하세요.

0 house
  (1) I see _____a house_____ on the hill. (a)
  (2) I see _____two houses_____ on the hill. (two)

1 puppy
  (1) There is _____ in my house. (a)
  (2) There are _____ in my house. (three)

2 scarf
  (1) She has _____. (a)
  (2) She has _____. (many)

3 child
  (1) _____ is in the pool. (a)
  (2) _____ are in the pool. (four)

4 potato
  (1) She needs _____. (a)
  (2) She needs _____. (three)

C ( ) 안에서 알맞은 말을 고르세요.

0   They are (⟨sheep⟩, sheeps).

1   The (man, men) are soldiers.

2   Seoul is a (city, cities).

3   There are two (monkies, monkeys) in the tree.

4   I have two (toothbrush, toothbrushes).

5   Fishermen catch (fish, fishes).

6   These (pant, pants) are too tight.

7   She has a pair of (glove, gloves).

8   It is a funny (story, stories).

9   A rabbit has long (ear, ears) and a short (tail, tails).

D ( ) 안의 말을 이용하여 우리말을 영어로 옮기세요.

0   정원에 나무 세 그루가 있다. (tree)

→ There are _____three trees_____ in the garden.

1   그 소년은 장난감이 많이 있다. (a lot of, toy)

→ The boy has _____.

2   나는 하루에 세 번 이를 닦는다. (tooth)

→ I brush my _____ three times a day.

3   책장에 사전 두 개가 있다. (dictionary)

→ There are _____ on the shelf.

4   Mike는 구두 한 켤레가 필요하다. (pair, shoe)

→ Mike needs _____.

A 다음 중 셀 수 없는 명사를 고르세요.

0	ⓐ spoon	ⓑ table	✓ⓒ milk	ⓓ bottle
1	ⓐ money	ⓑ coin	ⓒ watch	ⓓ knife
2	ⓐ ant	ⓑ bike	ⓒ chair	ⓓ hope
3	ⓐ dish	ⓑ snow	ⓒ toy	ⓓ house
4	ⓐ map	ⓑ flower	ⓒ hat	ⓓ juice
5	ⓐ apple	ⓑ math	ⓒ tree	ⓓ computer
6	ⓐ mouse	ⓑ photo	ⓒ onion	ⓓ meat
7	ⓐ homework	ⓑ school	ⓒ bag	ⓓ teacher
8	ⓐ city	ⓑ library	ⓒ park	ⓓ Seoul

B 보기에서 알맞은 말을 골라 문장을 완성하세요. (단, 한 번씩만 쓸 것)

보기	water	coffee	soap	bread
	Coke	rice	paper	cheese

0 I want a glass of _____water_____.

1 She has a bowl of _____ for dinner.

2 There is a loaf of _____ on the table.

3 I need a pen and a piece of _____.

4 I put a slice of _____ on my bread.

5 My family uses a bar of _____ a month.

6 Mom drinks a cup of _____ every morning.

7 He wants a can of _____ and some potato chips.

C ( ) 안의 말을 이용하여 문장을 완성하세요.

0   Mr. Rogers has two _____ *sons* _____. (son)

1   Good _____ is important. (health)

2   I drink _____ in the afternoon. (tea)

3   Bill has many good _____. (friend)

4   She puts some _____ in her coffee. (sugar)

5   Thank you for your _____. (advice)

6   _____ is my favorite sport. (baseball)

7   The students ask a lot of _____. (question)

8   We have five _____ of _____. (piece, pizza)

9   I need two _____ and some _____. (egg, butter)

D ( ) 안의 말을 이용하여 우리말을 영어로 옮기세요.

0   그는 매월 많은 돈을 저금한다. (money)

   → He saves a lot of _____ *money* _____ every month.

1   나는 신선한 공기가 필요하다. (air)

   → I need some fresh _____.

2   내 신발에 모래가 좀 들어갔다. (sand)

   → I have some _____ in my shoes.

3   우리에게 주스 세 병이 있다. (juice)

   → We have _____.

4   책상 위에 초콜릿 두 상자가 있다. (chocolate)

   → There are _____ on the desk.

UNIT 03 부정관사 A/An The Indefinite Articles *A/An*

A 빈칸에 a, an 중 알맞은 것을 쓰세요.

0 She is _____an_____ actress.

1 I have _____ good idea.

2 They live in _____ igloo.

3 _____ hand has five fingers.

4 He is _____ honest man.

5 Sally wears _____ uniform.

6 Lucy has _____ umbrella.

7 This is _____ expensive watch.

8 I get my hair cut once _____ month.

9 My brother has _____ iguana as a pet.

B 보기에서 알맞은 말을 골라 a, an과 함께 써서 문장을 완성하세요.

보기	chef	~~dentist~~	mechanic	pilot	writer	architect

0 Judy treats people's teeth. She is _____a dentist_____.

1 Peter flies an airplane. He is _____.

2 George fixes cars. He is _____.

3 Mike cooks food at a restaurant. He is _____.

4 Kate writes books. She is _____.

5 Clair designs buildings. She is _____.

C ( ) 안에서 알맞은 말을 고르세요. (X는 필요 없음을 뜻함)

0　I want (a, an, X) tuna sandwich.

1　Sam is (a, an, X) nice person.

2　These are (a, an, X) comfortable chairs.

3　That is (a, an, X) interesting book.

4　Do you want some (a, an, X) cookies?

5　This is my friend (a, an, X) Cindy.

6　Tom needs (a, an, X) new computer.

7　There is (a, an, X) milk in the refrigerator.

8　I have (a, an, X) sister and two brothers.

9　He drinks (a, an, X) orange juice every morning.

D ( ) 안의 말을 이용하여 우리말을 영어로 옮기세요.

0　식탁 위에 컵이 한 개 있다. (cup)

　　→ There is _____a cup_____ on the table.

1　Mary는 매일 아침 사과 한 개를 먹는다. (apple)

　　→ Mary eats _____ every morning.

2　일주일은 7일이다. (week)

　　→ _____ has seven days.

3　나는 매일 한 시간씩 영어를 공부한다. (hour)

　　→ I study English for _____ every day.

4　하와이는 아름다운 섬이다. (beautiful, island)

　　→ Hawaii is _____.

UNIT 04 정관사 The The Definite Article *The*

A ( ) 안에서 알맞은 말을 고르세요.

0 He is (a, the) good student.

1 (A, The) soup is salty.

2 (An, The) owl is a bird.

3 Open (a, the) window, please.

4 I know a girl. (A, The) girl is from Canada.

5 We have breakfast in (a, the) kitchen.

6 Is (a, the) tomato a vegetable?

7 (A, The) name of the boy is Tom.

8 Christmas comes once (a, the) year.

9 This is (an, the) easy question.

B 빈칸에 the, X 중 알맞은 것을 쓰세요. (X는 필요 없음을 뜻함)

0 ___The___ woman is my teacher.

1 We eat _____ lunch in the cafeteria.

2 Ann listens to _____ radio in the morning.

3 _____ sun is very hot today.

4 My father plays _____ golf on Sundays.

5 Peter goes to work by _____ subway.

6 Your keys are on _____ table.

7 My favorite subject is _____ science.

8 People in Mexico speak _____ Spanish.

9 The kids go to _____ bed around 9 o'clock.

C 밑줄 친 부분을 바르게 고치세요.

0   I live in the Seoul.   →   Seoul

1   She studies the history at university.   →

2   A girl is pretty.   →

3   We learn an English at school.   →

4   Robert goes to work by the car.   →

5   Betty has a dinner at home.   →

6   They play the soccer after school.   →

7   I practice piano every day.   →

8   He often skips a breakfast.   →

9   There is a rainbow in a sky.   →

D ( ) 안의 말을 이용하여 우리말을 영어로 옮기세요.

0   우리는 특별한 날에 그 식당에 간다. (restaurant)

→ We go to _____the restaurant_____ on special days.

1   달은 밤에 빛난다. (moon)

→ _____ shines at night.

2   나는 인터넷을 매일 사용한다. (Internet)

→ I use _____ every day.

3   Sally는 수학과 과학을 잘 한다. (math, science)

→ Sally is good at _____ and _____.

4   Mike는 밴드에서 기타를 연주한다. (guitar)

→ Mike plays _____ in a band.

A 밑줄 친 말을 대명사로 바꿔 쓰세요.

0	<u>Mr. Brown</u> is my history teacher.	→	He
1	I know <u>Sally's brother</u>.	→	
2	<u>Their house</u> is big.	→	
3	Max is <u>the dog's</u> name.	→	
4	My father uses <u>the computer</u>.	→	
5	<u>You and I</u> are 16 years old.	→	
6	<u>You and your brother</u> are tall.	→	
7	I know <u>Jane and Jane's sister</u>.	→	
8	John loves <u>his wife</u>.	→	
9	The classroom is <u>our classroom</u>.	→	

B ( ) 안에서 알맞은 말을 고르세요.

0 (I, My, Mine) am a student.

1 Hi. (I, My, Mine) name is Dave.

2 (You, Your, Yours) new coat is pretty.

3 Judy likes her job. She enjoys (it, its, them) a lot.

4 I have an uncle. (He, His, Him) lives in Canada.

5 Greg is very kind. He always helps (we, our, us).

6 The book on the table is (he, his, her).

7 The car is our neighbors'. It is (us, ours, theirs).

8 The (boy's, boys') names are Paul and Chris.

9 The shop sells (men's, mens') shoes.

C ( ) 안의 말을 적절한 형태로 바꾸어 문장을 완성하세요.

0   Kevin is my friend. I like _____him_____. (he)

1   The restaurant is famous for _____ fresh seafood. (it)

2   Stella looks like _____ grandmother. (she)

3   These are my mom's shoes. They are _____. (she)

4   Mr. Kim is a teacher. _____ teaches art. (he)

5   _____ apartment is on the first floor. (they)

6   Joe and _____ like sports. (I)

7   My parents understand _____ well. (I)

8   Here are some cookies for _____. (you)

9   Their house is in the country. _____ is in the city. (we)

D 우리말과 뜻이 같도록 빈칸에 알맞은 말을 쓰세요.

0   그는 내 사촌이다.

→ _____He_____ is my cousin.

1   David는 나에게 자주 전화한다.

→ David often calls _____.

2   나는 그들의 음악을 좋아한다.

→ I like _____ music.

3   그 분홍색 신발은 그녀의 것이다.

→ The pink shoes are _____.

4   그것은 Amy의 인형이다.

→ It is _____ doll.

06 This, That, It *This, That, It*

A ( ) 안에서 알맞은 말을 고르세요.

0 ((This), These) is our house.

1 (This, It) is sunny today.

2 (This, These) are my friends.

3 (This, These) coffee is hot.

4 (This, It) is Saturday today.

5 (That, Those) gloves are Jake's.

6 (This, These) is my favorite T-shirt.

7 (This, These) questions are difficult.

8 (That, Those) man over there is my father.

9 (That, It) is 10 kilometers from here to the beach.

B 밑줄 친 it의 쓰임이 나머지 둘과 다른 것을 고르세요.

0 ⓐ It is summer.   ⓑ It is June 1.   ✓ⓒ It's mine.

1 ⓐ It is my school.   ⓑ It is cool today.   ⓒ It's bright in this room.

2 ⓐ It is 10:30.   ⓑ It is Saturday.   ⓒ It is a gift for you.

3 ⓐ It is 1km to the station. ⓑ It is very cute.   ⓒ It is December 25.

4 ⓐ It is fine today.   ⓑ It is noon.   ⓒ It is 1,000 won.

5 ⓐ It is a cat.   ⓑ It is my birthday.   ⓒ It is true.

6 ⓐ It is a nice car.   ⓑ It is six thirty.   ⓒ I like it very much.

7 ⓐ It is a bear.   ⓑ It tastes good.   ⓒ It is October.

8 ⓐ It is the 1st of April. ⓑ It is an album.   ⓒ It is cheap.

C 보기에서 알맞은 말을 골라 문장을 완성하세요. (단, 한 번씩만 쓸 것)

보기	~~this~~	these	it

0   ____This____ is my sister Ann.

1   _____ is spring!

2   _____ are beautiful flowers.

보기	that	those	it

3   I like _____ shoes.

4   _____ is 8 o'clock.

5   _____ is a great movie.

D 우리말과 뜻이 같도록 빈칸에 알맞은 말을 쓰세요.

0   이분은 김 선생님이다.

→ _____This_____ is Mr. Kim.

1   저것은 멋진 사진이다.

→ _____ is a nice picture.

2   이 엽서들 좀 봐.

→ Look at _____ postcards.

3   저것들은 나의 책이다.

→ _____ are my books.

4   밤에는 춥고 바람이 많이 분다.

→ _____ is cold and windy at night.

Be동사의 현재형 Present Simple: *Be*

A 빈칸에 알맞은 be동사의 현재형과 줄임말을 각각 쓰세요.

0   He _____is_____ my father.   →   ____He's____ my father.

1   You _____ a nice person.   →   _____ a nice person.

2   She _____ a great singer.   →   _____ a great singer.

3   It _____ my pet dog.   →   _____ my pet dog.

4   I _____ tired.   →   _____ tired.

5   They _____ at school.   →   _____ at school.

6   We _____ from England.   →   _____ from England.

B 빈칸에 be동사 현재형의 부정형과 그 줄임말을 각각 쓰세요.

0   I ____am not____ sleepy.   →   ____I'm not____ sleepy.

1   We _____ in India.   →   We _____ in India.

2   They _____ my sisters.   →   They _____ my sisters.

3   You _____ late.   →   You _____ late.

4   He _____ a pilot.   →   He _____ a pilot.

5   It _____ funny.   →   It _____ funny.

6   That _____ a lion.   →   That _____ a lion.

7   The lake _____ deep.   →   The lake _____ deep.

8   The apples _____ sweet.   →   The apples _____ sweet.

9   My friends _____ here.   →   My friends _____ here.

C ( ) 안의 말과 be동사를 이용하여 현재형 의문문과 대답을 완성하세요.

0   A: _____Is he_____ a P.E. teacher? (he)

   B: Yes, _____he is_____ .

1   A: _____ a city? (Africa)

   B: No, _____ .

2   A: _____ at the park? (the boys)

   B: Yes, _____ .

3   A: _____ your jacket? (this)

   B: No, _____ .

4   A: _____ a good friend? (I)

   B: Yes, _____ .

D ( ) 안의 말을 이용하여 우리말을 영어로 옮기세요.

0   나는 12살이다. (I)

   → _____I am_____ 12 years old.

1   그들은 교실에 없다. (they)

   → _____ in the classroom.

2   너는 지금 바쁘니? (you)

   → _____ busy now?

3   이 컴퓨터는 빠르지 않다. (This computer)

   → _____ fast.

4   너희 부모님은 엄격하시니? (your parents)

   → _____ strict?

There is/are *There is/are*

A ( ) 안에서 알맞은 말을 고르세요.

0 There (**is**, are) a pond in the park.

1 There (is, are) pictures on the wall.

2 There (is, are) some milk in the fridge.

3 There (is, are) a lamp in the corner.

4 There (is, are) two mosquitoes in the room.

5 There (is, are) a movie theater near my house.

6 There (is, are) three kittens on the sofa.

7 There (is, are) a baseball glove in the box.

8 There (is, are) five people in my family.

9 There (is, are) some snow on the ground.

B 빈칸에 isn't 또는 aren't를 넣어 문장을 완성하세요.

0 There _____ *isn't* _____ any orange juice in the shop.

1 There _____ any spoons and forks on the table.

2 There _____ a library in this school.

3 There _____ many cars in the parking lot.

4 There _____ a copy machine in the office.

5 There _____ any toilet paper in the bathroom.

6 There _____ any flowers in the garden.

7 There _____ many people in the park.

8 There _____ any food in the fridge.

9 There _____ any bread at the bakery.

B 빈칸에 Is there 또는 Are there을 넣어 질문을 완성하고 알맞은 대답을 고르세요.

0 ___Is there___ any ice cream? ⓐ Yes, there are. ✓ⓑ No, there isn't.

1 _____ kids in the playground? ⓐ Yes, there are. ⓑ No, there isn't.

2 _____ a cup on the table? ⓐ Yes, there is. ⓑ No, there aren't.

3 _____ any sugar in the jar? ⓐ Yes, there are. ⓑ No, there isn't.

4 _____ birds in the tree? ⓐ Yes, there is. ⓑ No, there aren't.

5 _____ a chair in this room? ⓐ Yes, there is. ⓑ No, there aren't.

6 _____ vegetables in the shop? ⓐ Yes, there are. ⓑ No, there isn't.

7 _____ elephants in Africa? ⓐ Yes, there are. ⓑ No, there isn't.

8 _____ apples in the basket? ⓐ Yes, there is. ⓑ No, there aren't.

9 _____ a test this week? ⓐ Yes, there are. ⓑ No, there isn't.

D 우리말과 뜻이 같도록 빈칸에 알맞은 말을 쓰세요.

0 식탁 위에 빈 병이 한 개 있다.

→ ___There is___ an empty bottle on the table.

1 내 주머니에 돈이 조금 있다.

→ _____ some money in my pocket.

2 농장에 소가 많이 있다.

→ _____ many cows on the farm.

3 프린터기에 종이가 하나도 없다.

→ _____ any paper in the printer.

4 주전자에 뜨거운 물이 있니?

→ _____ hot water in the kettle?

09 일반동사의 현재형 1 Present Simple 1

A 주어진 동사의 3인칭 단수 현재형을 쓰세요..

0	eat	–	eats	10	run	–	
1	meet	–		11	jog	–	
2	jump	–		12	teach	–	
3	wash	–		13	miss	–	
4	finish	–		14	study	–	
5	love	–		15	cry	–	
6	know	–		16	enjoy	–	
7	have	–		17	do	–	
8	listen	–		18	fix	–	
9	want	–		19	come	–	

B ( ) 안에서 알맞은 말을 고르세요.

0 Sandy (swim, swims) well.

1 My brother and I (like, likes) pizza.

2 The boy (play, plays) basketball very well.

3 My grandmother (go, goes) to church on Sundays.

4 I (speak, speaks) English and Chinese.

5 My sister (wake, wakes) me up every morning.

6 The bank (close, closes) at 4 o'clock.

7 My aunt (live, lives) in Florida.

8 Ben and Clara (read, reads) a lot of books.

9 Mrs. Brown (smile, smiles) all the time.

C ( ) 안에 주어진 동사의 현재형을 써서 문장을 완성하세요.

0   Kelly _____*drinks*_____ tea in the afternoon. (drink)

1   Mom _____ eggs for me every morning. (fry)

2   The men _____ in this building. (work)

3   Mr. White _____ two children. (have)

4   We _____ milk from cows. (get)

5   Most people _____ holidays. (like)

6   Bats and owls _____ for food at night. (hunt)

7   Henry _____ Christmas with his family. (spend)

8   Mary _____ art class on Wednesdays. (have)

9   In summer, we _____ camping in the woods. (go)

D ( ) 안의 말을 이용하여 우리말을 영어로 옮기세요.

0   Paul과 Jane은 함께 학교에 다닌다. (go)

   → Paul and Jane _____*go*_____ to school together.

1   Rosa는 주말마다 요가를 한다. (do)

   → Rosa _____ yoga on weekends.

2   나의 형은 독일에서 음악을 공부한다. (study)

   → My brother _____ music in Germany.

3   새들은 겨울에 남쪽으로 날아간다. (fly)

   → Birds _____ south in winter.

4   여름에는 비가 많이 내린다. (rain)

   → It _____ a lot in summer.

UNIT 10 일반동사의 현재형 2 Present Simple 2

A ( ) 안에서 알맞은 말을 고르세요.

0   Peter (don't, (doesn't)) like broccoli.

1   My brother doesn't (sing, sings) well.

2   These pants (don't, doesn't) fit me.

3   My grandfather (don't, doesn't) smoke anymore.

4   (Do, Does) you like action movies?

5   (Do, Does) your father drive to work?

6   (Do, Does) Tim and Sue feed their pets?

7   We (don't, doesn't) play soccer on Sundays.

8   Does it (snow, snows) in California?

9   The students (don't, doesn't) have any classes today.

B ( ) 안의 말을 이용하여 현재형 부정문을 완성하세요. (줄임말을 쓸 것)

0   Chris _____ doesn't watch _____ TV. (watch)

1   They _____ Korean. (speak)

2   My sister _____ long hair. (have)

3   Henry _____ to school. (walk)

4   I _____ the answer. (know)

5   This mushroom soup _____ good. (taste)

6   Kimberly _____ many books. (read)

7   Dave and Sue _____ school uniforms. (wear)

8   The bus _____ downtown. (go)

9   Giraffes _____ meat. (eat)

C ( ) 안의 말을 이용하여 현재형 의문문과 대답을 완성하세요.

0 A: _____Do_____ you _____keep_____ a diary? (keep)

   B: No, _____I don't_____.

1 A: _____ I _____ well? (dance)

   B: Yes, _____.

2 A: _____ the girls _____ football? (like)

   B: No, _____.

3 A: _____ Mr. Smith _____ science? (teach)

   B: Yes, _____.

4 A: _____ the dog _____ loudly? (bark)

   B: No, _____.

D ( ) 안의 말을 이용하여 우리말을 영어로 옮기세요.

0 나는 매운 음식을 좋아하지 않는다. (like)

   → I _____don't like_____ spicy food.

1 Fred는 그의 방을 청소하지 않는다. (clean)

   → Fred _____ his room.

2 우리 부모님은 여행을 많이 하지 않는다. (travel)

   → My parents _____ much.

3 Mary와 Jane은 서로 아는 사이이니? (know)

   → _____ Mary and Jane _____ each other?

4 너희 학교는 수영장이 있니? (have)

   → _____ your school _____ a swimming pool?

Be동사 vs. 일반동사 Verbs in the Present Simple

A ( ) 안에서 알맞은 말을 고르세요.

0 Bill (get, (gets)) up at 6:00 a.m. every day.

1 My friends (go, goes) camping every summer.

2 The girl (have, has) a pretty doll.

3 (Are, Do) they live in New York?

4 The dishes (aren't, don't) clean.

5 The cherry tomatoes (aren't, don't) expensive.

6 They (aren't, don't) grow flowers.

7 Jimmy (isn't, doesn't) at the library.

8 A: (Do, Are) spiders have eight legs? B: Yes, they (do, are).

9 A: (Do, Are) you a member of this club? B: No, I (don't, am not).

B 우리말과 일치하도록 빈칸에 알맞은 말을 쓰세요.

0	너는 연필을 가지고 있니?	→	_____Do_____ you have a pencil?
1	그녀는 요리를 잘 하니?	→	_____ she a good cook?
2	그들은 태국 음식을 좋아하니?	→	_____ they like Thai food?
3	그들은 변호사니?	→	_____ they lawyers?
4	그녀는 남동생이 있니?	→	_____ she have a brother?
5	그는 키가 크지 않다.	→	He _____ tall.
6	그와 나는 형제가 아니다.	→	He and I _____ brothers.
7	나는 거짓말을 하지 않는다.	→	I _____ tell lies.
8	그 토스터기는 잘 작동하지 않는다.	→	The toaster _____ work well.
9	Jones 씨 부부는 여기에 살지 않는다.	→	Mr. and Mrs. Jones _____ live here.

C 밑줄 친 부분을 바르게 고치세요.

0 Sumi <u>play</u> volleyball. → plays

1 Mike <u>isn't</u> study on Sundays. →

2 Mira and Namho <u>doesn't</u> walk to school. →

3 I <u>studies</u> English every day. →

4 <u>Does</u> she a middle school student? →

5 I <u>am have</u> homework today. →

6 He <u>isn't</u> listen to pop music. →

7 The books <u>don't</u> interesting. →

8 <u>Do</u> they at school right now? →

9 A: Do you know my phone number? →

   B: Yes, I <u>am</u>.

D ( ) 안의 말을 이용하여 우리말을 영어로 옮기세요.

0 이 차는 뜨겁지 않다. (hot)

   → This tea isn't hot.

1 Jake는 남의 말을 듣지 않는다. (listen)

   → Jake _____ to others.

2 그 나뭇잎들은 가을에 색을 바꾸지 않는다. (change)

   → The leaves _____ color in fall.

3 그들은 좋은 학생이니? (good, student)

   → _____

4 너는 미국 드라마를 보니? (watch)

   → _____ American dramas?

UNIT 12 장소를 나타내는 전치사 Prepositions of Place

A ( ) 안에서 알맞은 말을 고르세요.

0   The computer is (in, **on**) my desk.

1   There are two calendars (in, on) our classroom.

2   I meet my friend (at, on) the bus stop.

3   The moon is (above, on) the bridge.

4   There is a bench (at, under) the tree.

5   His office is between the post office (and, or) the bank.

6   Lucy sits next to (I, me) in class.

7   There is a taxi stand in front (of, from) the hospital.

8   My house is across (of, from) the gas station.

9   The remote control is (behind, behind of) the sofa.

B 빈칸에 at, on, in 중 알맞은 전치사를 넣어 문장을 완성하세요.

0   They live _____in_____ Seoul.

1   My father is _____ work.

2   Brian keeps his toys _____ the box.

3   There is a carpet _____ the floor.

4   Jane listens to the radio _____ her car.

5   There is someone _____ the door.

6   There aren't many cars _____ the road.

7   The dishes are _____ the shelf.

8   Sam finishes his homework _____ school.

9   We have beautiful roses _____ our garden.

C 보기에서 알맞은 말을 골라 문장을 완성하세요. (단, 한 번씩만 쓸 것)

| 보기 | ~~above~~ | between | across from |

0   The fireworks are _____ *above* _____ the river.

1   The bus stop is _____ the museum.

2   There is a fence _____ the two houses.

| 보기 | under | behind | in front of |

3   He spends a lot of time _____ the TV.

4   A backyard is a yard _____ a house.

5   My cat often hides _____ my bed.

D ( ) 안의 말을 이용하여 우리말을 영어로 옮기세요.

0   내 수프에 머리카락이 하나 있다. (my soup)

→ There is a hair _____ *in my soup* _____ .

1   우리 집은 세종로에 있다. (Sejong Street)

→ My house is _____ .

2   그 기차는 역마다 정차한다. (every station)

→ The train stops _____ .

3   램프는 침대 옆에 있다. (the bed)

→ The lamp is _____ .

4   경찰서는 병원과 서점 사이에 있다. (the hospital, the bookstore)

→ The police station is _____ .

UNIT 13 시간을 나타내는 전치사 Prepositions of Time

A ( ) 안에서 알맞은 말을 고르세요.

0   He goes for a walk (in, at) the evening.

1   We have soccer practice (at, on) Wednesdays.

2   The radio program starts (in, at) midnight.

3   Do you have a party (in, on) Christmas Day?

4   Sally studies math (during, for) one hour.

5   Do not make noise (during, for) the movie.

6   I sleep (to, until) 12 o'clock on weekends.

7   The shop is open from 10:00 a.m. (at, to) 8:00 p.m.

8   Ted does his homework (after, until) school.

9   My dad usually comes home (before, from) dinner.

B 빈칸에 at, on, in, X 중 알맞은 것을 쓰세요. (X는 필요 없음을 뜻함)

0   It is hot ____in____ summer.

1   We have dinner _____ 6 o'clock.

2   She doesn't eat late _____ night.

3   Rosa cleans her room _____ every day.

4   My birthday is _____ May 15.

5   They go on vacation _____ August.

6   The math test is _____ tomorrow.

7   I come home _____ the afternoon.

8   We go to the park _____ Sunday afternoon.

9   The soccer game is _____ next Friday.

C 보기에서 알맞은 말을 골라 문장을 완성하세요. (단, 한 번씩만 쓸 것)

| 보기 | ~~before~~ | for | until |

0 Our winter vacation starts _____before_____ Christmas.

1 They work _____ 8 hours a day.

2 I have classes _____ 2 o'clock today.

| 보기 | after | during | from |

3 Friday comes _____ Thursday.

4 It is cold _____ November to March.

5 There are many events _____ the festival.

D ( ) 안의 말을 이용하여 우리말을 영어로 옮기세요.

0 그는 저녁에는 한가하다. (the evening)

→ He is free _____in the evening_____.

1 Tom은 매일 30분 동안 운동을 한다. (30 minutes)

→ Tom exercises _____ every day.

2 우리는 식사 후에 후식을 먹는다. (a meal)

→ We have dessert _____.

3 기말고사는 다음 주에 시작한다. (next week)

→ Final exams start _____.

4 그는 밤에 일하고 낮 동안 잔다. (night, the day)

→ He works _____ and sleeps _____.

14 형용사 Adjectives

A 주어진 문장에서 형용사를 모두 찾아 동그라미 하세요.

0 This flower is (beautiful.)

1 That is a nice house.

2 I have an interesting book.

3 Is there anything special?

4 Soda is not good for your health.

5 My new neighbor is friendly.

6 That is a wonderful idea.

7 There is a white tiger at the zoo.

8 It is warm in spring.

9 The little girl has a lovely smile.

B 보기에서 알맞은 말을 골라 문장을 완성하세요. (단, 한 번씩만 쓸 것)

보기	big	dirty	happy	long
	poor	thick	wet	wide

0 The water is not clean. It is _____dirty_____ water.

1 Their house is not small. It is a _____ house.

2 The man is not rich. He is a _____ man.

3 The towels are not dry. They are _____ towels.

4 That movie is not short. It is a _____ movie.

5 The children are not sad. They are _____ children.

6 The river is not narrow. It is a _____ river.

7 The book is not thin. It is a _____ book.

C 보기에서 알맞은 말을 골라 대화를 완성하세요. (단, 한 번씩만 쓸 것)

보기	cold	full	heavy	old	~~tall~~

0   A: Your brother is very _____tall_____.

   B: Yes, he is a basketball player at his school.

1   A: Do you want this apple?

   B: No, thank you. I am _____.

2   A: There are twenty books in this box.

   B: I know. The box is _____.

3   A: Those shoes look _____.

   B: You are right. They're ten years old.

4   A: Do you like summer?

   B: No, I don't. I like _____ weather.

D ( ) 안의 말을 이용하여 우리말을 영어로 옮기세요.

0   그것은 이상한 이야기이다. (strange, story)

   → It is a _____strange story_____.

1   이 스웨터는 따뜻하다. (warm)

   → This sweater _____.

2   꽃병에 흰 장미 두 송이가 있다. (white, roses)

   → There are two _____.

3   그녀의 새 코트는 예쁘다. (new, coat)

   → Her _____ is pretty.

4   나는 맛있는 것을 원한다. (delicious, something)

   → I want _____.

15 부사 Adverbs

A ( ) 안에서 알맞은 말을 고르세요.

0   The man works (hard, hardly).

1   It is (bright, brightly) outside.

2   The orchestra plays (bad, badly).

3   The streets are (quiet, quietly) at night.

4   John is a (careful, carefully) student.

5   James has a (loud, loudly) voice.

6   Bats see (good, well) in the dark.

7   The woman looks (sad, sadly).

8   My dad often comes home (late, lately).

9   Cathy likes her (new, newly) job.

B ( ) 안의 말을 적절한 형태로 바꾸어 문장을 완성하세요.

0   She dresses ___beautifully___. (beautifully)

1   They smile _____. (happy)

2   My mom cooks _____. (fast)

3   My brother draws cartoons _____. (good)

4   Drive _____ on the highway. (careful)

5   The old woman walks very _____. (slow)

6   Sally talks _____ to other people. (polite)

7   You speak Korean _____. (perfect)

8   Do kangaroos jump _____? (high)

9   Do you come to school _____ every day? (early)

C 보기에서 알맞은 말을 골라 문장을 완성하세요. (단, 한 번씩만 쓸 것)

보기	very	~~well~~	loudly	quickly

0   Mary plays the piano very _____well_____.

1   Come here _____.

2   My grandfather snores _____ at night.

3   He is a _____ clever boy.

보기	easily	early	high	pretty

4   The airplane flies _____.

5   My sister learns languages _____.

6   We eat dinner _____.

7   The weather is _____ good today.

D ( ) 안의 말을 이용하여 우리말을 영어로 옮기세요.

0   우리 아빠는 노래를 못 부른다. (sing, bad)

    → My father _____sings badly_____.

1   Jim은 물건을 쉽게 고친다. (fix, things, easy)

    → Jim _____.

2   그 투수는 공을 빠르게 던진다. (throw, the ball, fast)

    → The pitcher _____.

3   그녀는 항상 시험을 잘 본다. (do, good)

    → She always _____ on tests.

4   나는 주말에는 늦게 일어난다. (get up, late)

    → I _____ on weekends.

UNIT 16 수량 형용사, 빈도부사 Quantifiers, Frequency Adverbs

A ( ) 안에서 알맞은 말을 고르세요.

0 He doesn't read (many, much) books.

1 He doesn't spend (many, much) money.

2 We get (many, a lot of) rain in summer.

3 There are (few, little) flowers in the garden.

4 There is (few, little) water in the bottle.

5 She speaks (a few, a little) English.

6 She knows (a few, a little) English words.

7 I need (any, some) new shoes.

8 There isn't (any, some) butter in the refrigerator.

9 Do you want (any, some) chocolate?

B 보기에서 알맞은 말을 골라 문장을 완성하세요. (단, 한 번씩만 쓸 것)

보기	few	a few	little	a little

0 Excuse me. I have _____a few_____ questions.

1 Stella is very busy. She has _____ free time.

2 The actor isn't famous at all. _____ people know him.

3 I have _____ money. Let's get some snacks.

C ( ) 안의 말을 알맞은 곳에 넣어 문장을 다시 쓰세요.

0 Mr. Kim is nice to his students. (always)

→ _____ Mr. Kim is always nice to his students. _____

1 It is cold in December. (usually)

→ _____

2 Do you meet Judy? (often)

→ _____

3 I make mistakes. (sometimes)

→ _____

4 She drinks coffee at night. (never)

→ _____

D ( ) 안의 말을 이용하여 우리말을 영어로 옮기세요.

0 지하철에 사람들이 많이 있다. (people)

→ There are ___ a lot of[many] people ___ on the subway.

1 호수에 물이 거의 없다. (water)

→ There is _____ in the lake.

2 Sam은 학교에 친구가 하나도 없다. (friend)

→ Sam doesn't have _____ at school.

3 그의 조언은 항상 도움이 된다. (always, helpful)

→ His advice _____.

4 그녀는 절대 거짓말을 하지 않는다. (tell)

→ She _____ lies.

MEMO

MEMO

MEMO

Grammar Mate 1

Grammar Mate is a three-level grammar series for intermediate learners. This series is designed to help students understand basic English grammar with various step-by-step exercises. All chapters offer writing exercises to strengthen students' writing abilities and grammatical accuracy as well as review tests to prepare them for actual school tests. This series can be used by teachers in the classroom, by tutors teaching a small group of students, and by students for self-study purposes. With this series, students will improve their confidence in English. In addition, they will develop a solid foundation in English grammar to prepare themselves for a more advanced level.

Key Features

- Core basic English grammar
- Easy, clear explanations of grammar rules and concepts
- Plenty of various step-by-step exercises
- Writing exercises to develop writing skills and grammatical accuracy
- Comprehensive tests to prepare for actual school tests
- Workbook for further practice

Components Student Book | Workbook | Answer Key

Online Resources : www.darakwon.co.kr

Vocabulary Lists & Tests | Sentence Lists & Tests | Extra Exercises | Midterm & Final Exams

Grammar Mate Series

- QR코드를 통해 본 교재의 상세 정보 및 부가학습 자료를 이용하실 수 있습니다.
- 다락원 홈페이지에서 모바일 PC 기반 신개념 외국어 전자책인 DV BOOK을 이용하실 수 있습니다.